# With a  Psalm in My Heart

Gerri Johnson

Copyright © 2019

DAN AND GERRI JOHNSON

PO Box 9

Harrison, Tennessee 37412

gerrisbookcorner@gmail.com

Telephone: 865-230-7217

ISBN: 978-0-98443833-4

COVER DESIGN

Bryan Johnson

PAGE LAYOUT AND DESIGN

Linda Stubblefield

PROOFREADER

Rena Fish

*All Scripture references used in this book are from the King James Bible.*

Printed and Bound in the United States

# Introduction

I AM NOT a theologian. This book is not meant to be a deep study of the book of Psalms. Neither is it meant to include comments on all of the verses in each psalm.

This book is meant to give a few devotional thoughts on one or more verses in each Psalm. My idea in writing this book was for a daily devotional, considering one Psalm a day. But it can also be read as a whole—all at once or at least several chapters at a time. However you decide to read it, since I did not include the actual Psalm in the book, I suggest you read the corresponding Psalm from your Bible and then read the devotional thoughts.

I wrote this book from a woman's point of view, especially with Christian women in mind, although men are certainly welcome to read it too. I trust each of my readers will receive a blessing as I did in looking at each Psalm and applying it to my life. I trust and pray my readers will live each day with a Psalm in their heart.

# Enhance
## *your reading experience!*

Free Journal Page!

I hope you will enjoy your dive into the Psalms as much as I have enjoyed mine. It is my favorite Old Testament book. If you enjoy taking notes or writing down thoughts, I have something that you might enjoy.

If you are interested in a free journal page that you can print out and fill in for each of the psalms, please copy the link on this page in your browser. It will give you suggested questions to help you think and get more out of each devotional, with space to record your responses.

Happy reading and meditating as you go through the book of Psalms! May the thoughts in this book help you go through each day with a psalm in your heart.

Go here to this site to sign up:
https://mailchi.mp/522323a5979f/withapsalminmyheart

Questions? Reach me at gerrisbookcorner@gmail.com.

# Contents

# 𝔓salm 1

PSALM ONE provides the reader with two visual images: 1) a tree planted beside a river, and 2) chaff blowing in the wind. With so many types of trees, I want you to visualize the one I envision, with huge branches extending out over the banks and the water. The tree I picture is one of elegance and strength. The chaff, on the other hand, has no substance and is blown about by any wind. To which one would you rather be compared?

The ungodly, of course, are the unsaved. Sometimes we Christians tend to be jealous of the ungodly or, at least, wonder why they sometimes seem to have so much more in terms of earthly goods. But verse five states that they will not stand in the judgment. All of their possessions will not help them when they stand before God. They may enjoy what they have for a fleeting time on this earth, but then it is gone—like the chaff in the wind. Instead of enjoying eternity, they will suffer for eternity.

How much better it is to be counted with the righteous! Unfortunately, we will not be like that beautiful tree along the riverbank simply because we have trusted Jesus as our Saviour. In order to be blessed and to have the prosperous life promised by God in verse three, we should follow these guidelines:

1) **Don't walk in the counsel of the ungodly.** To whom do you go for advice or help in making decisions? Believers should not seek advice from unsaved people who know nothing of God's principles for life. The unsaved possess a world view that does not include godly, Christian principles. We need to be careful not to allow their mindset to influence us.

2) **Don't stand in the way of sinners.** I see a progression taking place in this verse. "Standing" with someone seems to indicate two or more people building a closer relationship by spending more time together as opposed to walking somewhere together. Obviously, we cannot completely avoid the ungodly. We interact with them in our daily life. Of course, we have the responsibility of sharing the gospel with them, but we should not develop close relationships with them.

II Corinthians 6:14 says, *"Be ye not unequally yoked together with unbelievers...."* This verse is often used to reprove someone's dating and marrying an unsaved person. This usage is correct; however, this verse also addresses other relationships. Those with whom we spend an abundance of time and with whom we associate should not be unsaved people, for *"...what fellowship hath righteousness with unrighteousness?"*

3) **Don't sit in the seat of the scornful.** To be *scornful* means to "mock, have in derision, scoff." Some synonyms include *disdain*, which means to "consider or reject as beneath oneself," and *despise*, which means to "regard as unworthy." Often in an attempt to make himself look better, a scornful person will criticize and belittle others. Scorning involves the

improper use of the mouth God has given us to use for His purposes! Watch what you say!

The progression continues: rather than standing around, the word *sit* is used. Sitting implies enjoying an even closer relationship or spending more time with the one who is a scorner. How dangerous that can be! If we are not already scornful, the scorner's attitude will soon rub off on us! A bad apple ruins the rest of the basket—not the other way around. We need to spend our time with people who have loving attitudes and use their words to build up, not tear down.

However, avoiding walking, standing, and sitting with scorners will not guarantee us prosperity or blessings. Verse two, which begins with "but," is the other side of the coin. We need to avoid wrong company and their counsel, but we must also substitute something else in its place. *"But his delight is in the law of the LORD; and in his law doth he meditate day and night."* Do we delight in God's Word? Do we let His Word permeate our being all day long? Psalm 119:14 says, *"I have rejoiced in the way of thy testimonies, as much as in all riches."*

Let us make His testimonies our desire and prayer. Only then can God bless us with true prosperity, and we will become like that beautiful tree beside the river.

# 𝔓salm 2

LISTENING TO today's news or reading the newspaper can be very disheartening. Seeing what is happening in our world is discouraging and humbling. Attempts are being made to remove God from our society. Bible reading and prayer have been wrested from our schools, and evolution is taught as fact—another way of removing God from our lives. Abortions are considered a woman's "right to choose," and homosexuality is considered an acceptable "alternative lifestyle."

A phrase in verse two, which says, *"the rulers take counsel together, against the LORD,"* seemingly and unhappily paints a picture of what is happening in America, as well as in other nations. God is continually being removed from public places, Christian views and philosophies are being ridiculed, and the ancient landmarks erected by a God-fearing society are being moved.

A future without God appears grim and bleak, but I love verse 4, which says, *"He that sitteth in the heavens shall laugh...."* God is not worried about the state of world events; the future He sees is full of promise. He knows what is happening, and He is still in complete control. He knows the final outcome, and if we know God's Word as Christians, so do we. Even in this Psalm, God indicates that the Lord will be victorious over evil rulers.

We might tend to become fearful or tremble over what the world seems to be coming to, but verse 11 includes something else to do with those emotions. *"Serve the* LORD *with fear, and rejoice with trembling."* We should not harbor an uncontrollable fear over the world situation, rather a worshipful fear of our great Lord. We should not tremble at the circumstances in the world; rather, we should tremble in awe of the Lord's might, rejoicing that He is our Saviour!

Don't be worried and uptight over the condition of the world today. Trust in the Lord, Who is in control of everything. The chapter concludes with this precious promise: *"...Blessed are all they that put their trust in him."* Trust Him!

# 𝔓salm 3

TWO VERSES especially caught my attention in the third
Psalm. Verse 5, *"I laid me down and slept; I awaked; for
the LORD sustained me."* When I was in seventh grade, I would
go to bed at night and wonder, "What will happen to me if I
die tonight?" Although my parents did not go to church at that
time, I loved church and always attended, so I knew the Bible
stories and had learned Bible verses. One night while thinking about what I had learned in church, I just took God at His
Word. I believed what He said about trusting in Jesus to save
me and forgive me of my sins, and I asked Him to forgive me.
Since that day I have had no more doubts. I can lie down each
night to sleep, knowing my life and soul are in His hands and
I am secure.

Just as we can be secure in our salvation and sure of having
a home in heaven, we can be sure God is with us and holding us in His hands every moment. As we travel through this
journey on earth, He is sustaining us. Why should we fear anything?

The second verse which captured my attention is verse 6, *"I*

*will not be afraid of ten thousands of people, that have set them-
selves against me round about."* Just as God watches over us as
we sleep and gives us rest at night, we can trust in Him during
the day—no matter how many enemies or frightful situations
confront us.

This verse makes me think of the story of Elisha and His
servant Gehazi at Dothan. The two of them were surrounded by thousands of the enemy, and Gehazi was fearful. Elisha
prayed that God would open His servant's eyes, and Gehazi
saw the mountains round about full of horses and chariots of
fire. What a sight that must have been! Maybe one of them was
the very chariot Elijah rode in when he was taken to heaven!

God was there in full force, as He is daily in our lives. We
cannot see Him with our physical eyes, so sometimes we feel
overwhelmed by what we do see. Thankfully, the psalmist said
in verse 4, *"I cried unto the LORD with my voice, and he heard
me out of His holy hill."* If we cry unto Him, He will hear us. So,
let's do as the psalmist did, and we will not have to fear by night
or by day.

# 𝔓salm 4

THE PSALMIST'S comment in verse 6a is interesting to me. *"There be many that say, Who will shew us any good?"* Have you ever wondered that? Do we sometimes complain, "Nothing good ever happens to me," as we look at the lives of others and see things that we think would be "good" for us— the better job, the nicer clothes, or a house that someone else has. How easy it is for us to complain or think that others are better off than we are.

Then the psalmist adds, *"LORD, lift thou up the light of thy countenance upon us,"* and provides the solution for complaining and discontent! Bask in the light of Jesus.

At this writing, we have had some cold days in Brazil. With no central heating or insulation in the houses, our house is often colder inside than out! Sometimes, when it is cold inside, I step outside to stand in the sun for a few minutes. The warmth feels so nice! The sun's rays on my face and body are comforting and soothing.

Jesus wants to do that for us when we are perhaps a little negative or simply don't understand why things do not seem to be going well in our eyes. We need to bask in the light of His countenance. How do we do that?

First, spend time in His Word. Psalm 119:105 says, *"Thy word is a lamp unto my feet, and a light unto my path."* Let God's light shine upon you through His Word. Psalm 119:28 says, *"My soul melteth for heaviness: strengthen thou me according unto the word."* When your heart is heavy and things do not seem good, get new strength from the Bible.

The second way to bask in His light is to walk with Him and talk with Him in prayer. Jesus said He was the light of the world. As we walk and talk with Him, that light will reflect on us and in us.

In the next verse, the psalmist says, *"Thou hast put gladness in my heart."* As we bask in the light of His countenance, our discontent and complaining will be replaced with gladness. The psalmist says it will be *"more than in the time that their corn and their wine increased"* (v. 7). This verse is speaking of the time of the most financial success—at the harvest when the investments and work of the year yield their increase. Our gladness as we look to the Lord for our contentment will be more than that of the world at their moments of greatest success, financial or otherwise.

Let's seek to be closer to Jesus. Let's bask in His light! Then watch discontentment give place to gladness.

# 𝔓salm 5

I N VERSE 3, the psalmist says, *"My voice shalt thou hear in the morning, O* LORD; *in the morning will I direct my prayer unto thee, and will look up."* David promised the Lord he would come to Him in the morning in prayer.

I do not know if you are a morning person or a night owl. I am not really a morning person, although if I have to get up early, I can. For a morning person to find extra time early in the day to meet with the Lord would likely be easier. But the truth is, all of us need to chisel out a little time in the morning to spend with the Lord. This time does not have to be your main time with Him. But the day goes so much better if we have found a few minutes to pray and read a verse—even if we pray while changing a diaper (if we have little ones)!

Verse 8 says, *"Lead me, O* LORD, *in thy righteousness because of mine enemies; make thy way straight before my face."* How can we expect to walk righteously in God's straight path if we do not ask Him in the morning to guide and direct our day and give us victory over our enemies. Oh, we might not have armies of soldiers as our enemies like David did, but we DO

---

have the world, the flesh, and the devil—and they will defeat us if we rely on our own strength for victory. Let's ask for God's help in the morning BEFORE we meet our enemies during the day!

Verse 11 says, *"But let all those that put their trust in thee rejoice: let them ever shout for joy, because thou defendest them."* Start your day with Him, and He will give victory. With the victory comes JOY. Maybe the reason so many Christians seem to lose their joy is that they forget to ask Him to defend them and give them the victory each day!

Joy comes as the Lord defends us. Often, we do not have the joy of seeing Him work in our defense. Instead, we come to Him to fix things after we mess them up and after we have allowed our enemies to defeat us!

Verse 12 says He will compass us as with a shield. Let's ask Him in the morning to be our shield and rejoice at the end of the day in His victory!

# ℘salm 6

ERSES ONE and 2 say, "*O LORD, rebuke me not in thine anger, neither chasten me in thy hot displeasure. Have mercy upon me, O LORD; for I am weak: O LORD, heal me; for my bones are vexed.*"

These two verses show our miserable human situation. We are weak, and because of that weakness, the Lord has to rebuke and chasten us. Oh, we may not rob banks or kill people, but have we ever robbed someone of His or her good name by gossiping or spreading rumors? Have we "killed" someone in our hearts through hatred, unforgiveness, or unkind words?

I find the phrase *"my bones are vexed"* very interesting. As I grow older, I am paying more and more attention to my bones. I have the beginning of osteoporosis, which I do not feel, but I suppose could cause problems in the future with easily broken bones. But I also have arthritis, which is what I DO feel! As I get out of bed in the morning or get out of a seat after sitting for a while, I feel like I need an oil can with me to spray on my joints to get them to work correctly. My left thumb, which I smashed in a car door as a child, healed nicely back then, but gives me much pain now. And it does not help that I am left-handed! So, yes, I find my bones very vexing.

But of more concern than our bones, verse 3 says, *"My soul is also sore vexed...."* In this Psalm, David is again talking about His enemies and how he wants to be free from them. Our problem, as I mentioned in discussing chapter 5, is not an army of men against us, but those old familiar enemies—the world, the flesh, and the devil. Our soul should be vexed if we allow them victory in our lives.

In verse 9, David said, *"The LORD hath heard my supplication; the LORD will receive my prayer."* He will hear mine too and yours. Let's call on Him for victory. I would love for my bones to stop "vexing" me, but much more important is to seek victory in my soul over whatever I am allowing to defeat me in my spiritual life.

# Psalm 7

THE FIRST concept I notice in this Psalm is Who David trusted in. He said in the first verse, *"O LORD my God, in thee do I put my trust."* Upon establishing his trust, he then asks God to save him from those who persecuted him. David did have enemies, and at times, he had people trying to kill him and take his life.

The Scripture reveals that David was a good soldier. But when he battled with Goliath and took the giant's life, he did not take matters into his own hands. He sought God and trusted in Him—not in his own strength or prowess.

In this Psalm, David reminds God how He could have killed King Saul, who unceasingly sought to kill David. Although David had opportunities to take Saul's life, he would not kill him because God had put Saul in the position of king. David left everything in God's hand and chose not to seek personal vengeance.

We probably do not have people literally seeking to take our life, but there may be those who seem to seek our harm, to defame us, to destroy our testimony, or in some other way inflict pain or cause us problems. We need to be like David and refrain from seeking personal vengeance, instead allowing God to resolve the problem in His own way.

David had done no wrong to cause Saul and others to turn on Him. He asked God to examine him and told God that if he had returned evil for evil, allowing His persecution would be acceptable.

Could we make the same statement to God? I am afraid that when someone "attacks" me, my first thought is often to seek retaliation. But David did not return evil for evil. His trust was in God to take care of him. In verse 10 he says, *"My defence is of God, which saveth the upright in heart."* How we need to learn from David, a man after God's own heart (Acts 13:22)! David mentions in verses 12 and 13 that God has his sword, bow, and instruments of death prepared for the unrighteous. He can defend us better than we can defend ourselves!

Verse 16 says, *"His mischief shall return upon his own head."* They will often bring their own destruction upon themselves! But if we return evil with evil and want vengeance, we may end up bringing problems upon ourselves. Let's allow God to take care of our enemies. When He works out the situation in His way, let's remember to thank and praise Him for it. David ends the Psalm by saying in verse 17, *"I will praise the LORD according to his righteousness: and will sing praise to the name of the LORD most high."*

# 𝔓salm 8

Verses three and four say, *"When I consider thy heavens, the work of thy fingers, the moon and the stars, which thou hast ordained; what is man that thou art mindful of him? and the son of man, that thou visitest him?"*

When I look at the sunny sky with beautiful clouds in the day, and the moon and stars at night, I find it almost overwhelming to realize that all that beauty represents only a small part of our amazing universe. The sun is merely a speck in our solar system, which is a small part of the Milky Way, which is only one of who knows how many other galaxies in the universe. Even with all our modern, cutting-edge technology, telescopes, satellites, and space travel, man has not begun to scratch the surface of knowing or understanding all of the intricacies of the universe.

Man really is nothing in comparison with the vastness of God's creation. Yet verse five states, *"For thou hast made him a little lower than the angels, and hast crowned him with glory and honour."* Even more, God gave us dominion over everything in our world! What a wonderful, loving God!

I will never understand how anyone can look at the complexity of all God created and think it came about by chance through evolution! Yet for the most part today, men explain God away and make science their god. Many scientists, and those whom they mislead, discard God and, therefore, God's Word, the Bible.

I heard an interesting story of how Matthew Murray decided to take God's Word literally, and as a result, he discovered a scientific truth. Verse seven mentions *"the paths of the sea,"* and when Mr. Murray read that verse, he decided to take God at His Word. Through analyzing the notes and logs of ship captains, he discovered the ocean currents.

I choose to let our wonderful, complex, amazing world point me to God and His Word! *"O LORD our LORD, how excellent is thy name in all the earth!"* (v. 9). How true!

# $\mathfrak{P}$salm 9

Does it ever appear to you that sometimes life just doesn't seem fair? I believe we all feel that way at times. The truth is that life is NOT always fair. When we see or face unfair situations, either in our lives or the lives of friends or loved ones, we sometimes have a tendency to want to make things right or seek vengeance for a wrong done. We might become frustrated or "out of sorts" over a situation when we cannot seem to make it right.

But verse 8 reminds us of an important fact. *"And he shall judge the world in righteousness, he shall minister judgment to the people in uprightness."* We need to remember two truths from this verse. First, God is the judge—not us. Second, God does not always act immediately, but He will act. We tend to want to see everything resolved right away, but God has a purpose for sometimes allowing difficulties and what seem like unfair situations. Because God is the judge, we need to leave matters in His hands and trust Him to work in His time.

Verses 9 and 10 say, *"The Lord also will be a refuge for the oppressed, a refuge in times of trouble. And they that know thy name will put their trust in thee: for thou, Lord, hast not forsaken them that seek thee.*" When life doesn't seem fair, we have somewhere to turn. When we are oppressed or in trouble, He is our refuge. Sometimes we remember that fact after we have complicated a situation by trying to resolve it ourselves or after we have given ourselves ulcers worrying about the problem.

Let's turn these situations over to God immediately. Let's remember that He has NOT forsaken us—even if our problems are not resolved immediately. He is there to be our refuge in the time of trouble and distress. God never forsakes us.

Let's allow Him to be the judge and let Him resolve the issues in His own timing. Rest in the refuge of His arms and remember that He will never forsake us in any situation. He IS in complete control.

# 𝔓salm 10

𝕿HIS PSALM begins, *"Why standest thou afar off, O LORD? why hidest thou thyself in times of trouble?"* Do you ever feel like asking that question? Sometimes when we seem immersed in problems, the Lord seems very far away. Occasionally, we look at all the wickedness of the world around us and wonder where God is. The next verses of the Psalm talk about the wicked, using words such as *pride, covetous, cursing, deceit, fraud, mischief, vanity.* The phrase, *"murder the innocent,"* found in verse eight, makes me think of abortion, a horrendous practice that is becoming so accepted today.

Doesn't this series of words sound like a description of the world today? It seems easy to wonder where God is if we focus on all of the wickedness.

In verse four, the attitude of the wicked is revealed. *"The wicked, through the pride of his countenance, will not seek after God: God is not in all his thoughts."* Verse 11 says of the wicked person: *"He hath said in his heart, God hath forgotten: he hideth his face; he will never see it."* I believe these verses picture the world today. Many people do not even think about God, or if

WITH A PSALM IN MY HEART | 29

they do, they think He is not interested in their lives or does not care to interfere in the way they live.

But when life seems bleak and we do not see God at work, verse 14 reminds us, *"Thou hast seen it; for thou beholdest mischief and spite, to requite it with thy hand."* God does see, and the wicked will pay—whether in this life or the next.

I like verse 16, which says, *"The LORD is King for ever and ever."* God is always in control. Believe it and trust the things of life to His hands.

Verse 17 continues, *"LORD, thou hast heard the desire of the humble."* Whether or not it seems like God is there, He does hear us. Believe it. Rest in Him. He hears our desires and prayers and will answer in His time. The words of the old song are still true:

God is still on the throne—
Almighty God is He,
And He cares for His own through all eternity.

He is mighty. He cares. Whether or not we can see that God is on the throne, it is true. Let's rest in Him in the middle of what seems like chaos!

# Psalm 11

MORE AND more wickedness seems to be in the world today, and the wicked always seem to be fighting a spiritual battle against righteousness. Have you ever felt like you could not face the battle and wanted to turn and run like a puppy with His tail tucked under? Psalm 11:1 gives the illustration of another animal—a bird flying away into the mountain, fleeing from the arrows of a predator.

Verse three asks a rhetorical question: *"If the foundations be destroyed, what can the righteous do?"* Without a foundation, we cannot have victory over the wicked, BUT the saved DO have a foundation. That foundation is Jesus—our Saviour and our Rock. Because of that solid foundation, we do not have to flee!

I love verse four, which says, *"The LORD is in his holy temple, the LORD's throne is in heaven...."* He is always there for us. He is never away on a trip when we need Him! We can be like a little child who thinks, *Daddy's home. Everything is okay.*

The second part of verse four tells us His eyes behold us and His eyelids try us. We can show so much through our eyes! Mothers often wear the look of *Watch out! I see what you are doing!* or *I am watching; everything is okay,* or *I love you, and I am with you.* Sometimes a parent may give that stare that says, *I am waiting to see what you will do!*

God's eyes are on us in the same way earthly parents watch their children. His watchful eye protects us from danger, but He sometimes watches to see how we will react to difficult situations. If we remember that He is our foundation and is available for us, we can react with confidence in His help. We do not need to turn tail and run or flee. God is with us, and He is for us. As verse seven says, *"his countenance doth behold the upright."*

# $\mathcal{P}$salm 12

**W**HAT TROUBLE we can bring upon ourselves with our lips! The Bible addresses the use of our lips or tongues multiple times. The book of James says we cannot really tame them. Verses two and three address the following four problem areas that have to do with the tongue:

1) Speaking vanity
2) Flattering lips
3) Speaking with a double heart
4) Speaking proud things

Do we allow these behaviors to creep into our life—even though we try to control our tongue?

A common subject of jokes is that women talk a lot. Personally, I do not think we talk that much more than men, but what I think is beside the point! I am afraid finding ourselves speaking "vanity" with our neighbors or friends is much too easy to do. To me, that would include wasting our time talking about issues that simply do not matter. Nothing is wrong with simply having a good time and chitchatting at times, but we need to include in our conversations times of sharing blessings and spiritual truths or sharing the gospel with the unsaved. Vanity would also include spreading gossip, which we should cut completely from our conversations. Sometimes we gossip under the guise of being able to pray more knowledgeably for someone.

The psalmist mentions flattering lips twice. Everyone enjoys receiving a compliment, and we should try to give them freely to others. But flattery is simply not an honest compliment. One dictionary definition is "excessive, insincere praise." We should praise and compliment people for a job well done or something positive about them. But flattery usually includes the desire to manipulate the person or get something in return. Let us always be careful in how we treat others.

The next problem area the psalmist notes is those who speak with a double heart. To me, that would indicate being a hypocrite—thinking one way in our heart and saying the opposite. We can hide our feelings for a while, but at some point what is in our hearts will be reflected in what we say and in our attitude. So if we will get our heart in tune with the Lord, we will not need to worry about being double-hearted. Let's be honest and sincere in everything we say.

Lastly, the psalmist addresses speaking proud things. The world today seems to imply that we should watch out for ourselves and "do our own thing." That frame of mind can creep into the life of a Christian without his or her realizing its presence. Soon the person becomes an egotist, lifting up himself or herself and speaking with pride. But Jesus taught that whoever wanted to be first should become last. As Christians, we should be concerned about others—not about lifting up ourselves. If others praise us, let us accept their praise with humility. If they do not, let's not try to lift ourselves up with proud words. If we keep our mind focused on Jesus, we will be less likely to fall into the pit of pride.

Verse 4 contains an interesting phrase: *"Our lips are our own: who is lord over us?"* The Portuguese have a saying: "I am the owner of my own nose." That expression means much the same. In English, we would say, "I am my own boss." The problem is that as Christians, that statement is not true. We were bought with a price—the blood of Jesus. We belong to Him! Let us give ourselves anew to Him every day and let Him control everything—including our lips and tongue!

# ℙsalm 13

HAVE YOU ever felt like God has forgotten you? Oh, we still know He is there, but it seems at times that He is not present or working in our daily life. We feel depressed or distressed or overwhelmed with our problems and issues. We see no light at the end of the tunnel. In the thirteenth Psalm, the psalmist saw no light at the end of His tunnel. He spent the first part of the Psalm talking about how alone and forsaken he felt.

In verse three, he asks God to *"lighten mine eyes, lest I sleep the sleep of death."* This verse makes me think of Elijah, who saw a great victory against the prophets of Baal on Mt. Carmel. When things became difficult afterward and Jezebel sent him a message of her intent to have him killed, he told God he wanted to die.

When we feel despondent or depressed, like Elijah or David did, we can take steps to feel His presence. When troubles come and we do not feel God is there, we need to recognize that He IS there. David discovered the following steps and mentions them in verses five and six.

First, David trusted in God's mercy. Although He did not feel God's presence at the moment, He knew God was there and that He was merciful. He deposited his trust in that mercy.

Second, David rejoiced in God's salvation. If the only thing God did for us in our whole lives was to give us salvation and a home in heaven, that is enough reason to rejoice. This life, in comparison to eternity, will be over in the blink of an eye, and then we will spend forever in God's presence with no more problems or sorrows. So let us rejoice in our salvation, whether or not we feel like rejoicing. As we rejoice and dwell on what God did when He saved us, we will realize that God really is there and begin to feel His presence.

Then, the psalmist sang unto the Lord. Music has a powerful influence on us. So when you feel down, begin to sing spiritual songs to the Lord. Listen to good music that will uplift you and help put a song in your heart. The last phrase in verse six tells us why the psalmist sang: *"because he hath dealt bountifully with me."*

Think about all God has done for you in the past. I feel relatively sure He has done many things beyond just giving you salvation. Thinking about all of our blessings of the past will give us a song in our heart and will encourage us that He really IS there now—even if we do not feel His presence.

Let's trust His mercy, rejoice in our salvation, and sing praises to God. David did and turned from feeling forgotten by God to realizing how bountifully God had worked in his life.

He is working in yours—and mine too!

# $\mathfrak{P}$salm 14

$\mathbf{V}$ERSE ONE of this chapter has always captivated me. "*The fool hath said in his heart, There is no God.*" I cannot fathom how anyone can look at all the wonders of nature, the variety and intricacies of plants and flowers, and the array of animals from the huge exotic elephant to a tiny fluttering butterfly, not to mention smaller microscopic entities, and definitively say God did not create them.

I cannot fathom how anyone can look at the heavens, the sun and moon, the twinkling stars beyond our solar system and galaxy, and the beauty of the sunrise or sunset and say God did not set them all in order.

I cannot fathom how scientists who view the complexities of the vast universe through a telescope or the equal complexity of the minuscule particles they study under a microscope can attribute it all to evolution.

Yet that is what we see more and more of today. We are more "educated" today than at any other time in history, but humanism and theories such as evolution are the core of our secular educational system.

The problem is that man does not WANT to allow for or acknowledge a God because they would become responsible to Him. Therefore, modern man has removed God from creation and is now trying to take Him out of every aspect of their lives. The Bible and prayer have been taken out of schools.

But as much as all this saddens and frustrates me, I can understand it. Satan has blinded the eyes of the unsaved.

But what is really sad is that we, as Christians, often act as if there is no God. At least, we are not allowing Him to control our lives. We want to run our lives on our own.

We might never say that there is no God because we met Him personally at Calvary, but we do say, "No, God," when He asks to lead us and wants to show us His will.

Let's change our ways and not be fools in acting as if there is no God Who wants to lead and guide us!

# ℘salm 15

**V**ERSE one begins the Psalm by asking two questions: *"LORD, who shall abide in thy tabernacle? who shall dwell in thy holy hill?"* To me, it seems like the psalmist is asking, "Lord, who is Your good friend? Who is close to You?"

We all like having friends, and having a close friend we can always count on is especially refreshing. Jesus is the friend Who sticks closer than a brother, and He desperately wants to be that best friend to all of us, but many Christians do not feel that closeness.

The verses in the rest of the chapter contain the qualifications or qualities of the person who fits the description of one who is close to God. The list is quite lengthy, but some qualities stand out more. Verse two mentions walking *uprightly,* which means "blameless." Do we strive to live a pure life, using God's Word as a basis for our conduct and thoughts? To me, uprightness refers to our character and integrity. The verse continues with *"worketh righteousness."* After analyzing our inner life and our walk with God, we need to validate our works. We do not work for our salvation, but we work because we love God, because He is our friend, and because we want to please Him. Are we serving others or living for ourselves? If Jesus is our close friend, His love will flow through us and result in helping and serving others.

Verse three specifies backbiting. How we can be entangled by our tongues! Criticizing or condemning others if they do not think or act the way we do can be so easy. But even if we are right and they are wrong, it is God's job to deal with them—not ours. A close friend to Jesus will not backbite or commit evil against anyone.

Verse four says, *"In whose eyes a vile person is condemned; but he honoureth them that fear the Lord."* The condemning in this verse is not referring to speaking or doing evil against someone; rather, it is talking about not elevating and honoring those who do not honor God in their lives. Young people especially like to have heroes or "idols." Unfortunately, those idols are often rock stars or movie stars, who generally live a completely godless lifestyle. But even as we grow older, we can look to worldly people and make them our role models. If we want to be a close friend to Jesus, we will not elevate ungodly people in our minds. We will instead choose preachers, missionaries, and godly lay people as our personal role models.

The person who adds these qualities to His or her life, along with the others mentioned in this Psalm *"shall never be moved"* (v. 5). Have you ever felt like your life was crumbling around you? Let's strive to be Jesus' close friend so that even if problems come, we will be firmly grounded on the Rock (Jesus), and we will not be moved!

# Psalm 16

*I* ESPECIALLY like two verses in this Psalm. The last part of verse six says, *"yea, I have a goodly heritage."* My husband often refers to his Christian heritage. Everyone in his family is a professing Christian. His grandparents and great-grandparents on both sides were Christians. His parents reared his brothers and him in church, and they all are saved. Our children are all saved and serving the Lord. Our four sons are all missionaries, and our only daughter works with the deaf and is active in our home church. Some of our grandchildren have already surrendered to missions.

This legacy is not because we are anything special. We have simply strived to pass our *"goodly heritage"* on to our children and train them in the ways of the Lord. The goodness and blessings of God have worked mightily in our family.

If you have a *"goodly heritage,"* make sure you pass it on. Train your children in the ways of the Lord. But if you do not have a *"goodly heritage,"* do not despair! My husband emphasizes that even if you have a past that is less than stellar or even if no one in the family line is godly and trying to serve the

Lord, there is always a time to start! Be the first generation in a new line with a *"goodly heritage."* Strive to serve the Lord and train your children to do so; you can be the start of a family line that God can bless for generations to come!

Verse eleven says, *"Thou wilt shew me the path of life: in thy presence is fulness of joy; at thy right hand there are pleasures for evermore."* The three parts of this verse give us the secret of a *"goodly heritage."* We need to follow God's path—not the myriad of paths that the world offers and Satan tempts us with. Too many people, even Christians, want to walk the path of money, fame, or pleasure. Then we wonder why we do not have joy.

Joy is not found by seeking it; rather, it comes from walking the path of God's will for our lives and living in His presence. If we will do that, we will have the blessings of God and His joy in our lives. When this life is over, we will spend eternity with the Lord and have *"pleasures for evermore"!*

Let's either continue our goodly heritage and pass it on to future generations, or we can start a new "chain" of generations that God can bless because we are following His path.

# $\mathfrak{P}$salm 17

IN THIS Psalm, as in many others, David asks for help against his enemies—the wicked. In verse eight, he asks God, *"Keep me as the apple of the eye, hide me under the shadow of thy wings."*

This verse reminds me of the familiar illustration I love concerning a mother hen and her chicks. In the advent of a fire, she gathered her chicks under her wings. When the fire was extinguished, the mother hen had been burned to death. But under her protective wings, the baby chicks were alive and well! God protects us like that mother hen protected her chicks— only He is God, so we need never fear. He will not perish while protecting us from the fires of life. He is always available to protect us and help us when we call upon Him. David gave this assurance when He said in verse six, *"I have called upon thee, for thou wilt hear me, O God."*

But something came before that: David's heart had been freed from sin. Verse three says, *"Thou hast proved my heart; thou hast visited me in the night; thou hast tried me, and shalt find nothing."* His heart was clean, so he could freely claim God's protection.

So many times, we want God to help us or bless us. But we first need to make sure our heart is right with Him before we can expect His blessings. If, at the end of each day, we examine our heart and life for any unconfessed sin and take care of what we find and if God examines our heart in the night, He will find nothing amiss, as He did with David. Then we also can count on Him to help us.

Let's strive to constantly keep our hearts free of sin. I find the end of verse three interesting when David states, *"I am purposed that my mouth shall not transgress."*

We need to free ourselves of all sin, but the mouth is often our biggest problem. How many times do we criticize, complain, or in some other way use our mouth wrongly? Let's purpose like David not to transgress with our mouth!

Let's cleanse ourselves daily of all sins so we can know that God will hear us when we call on Him.

# 𝔓salm 18

D AVID HAD his share of enemies and difficult situations. But this Psalm shows that he knew where to go for help! In the first six verses, he says he will call upon the Lord, confident he will be helped. He calls the Lord several names, including his rock, fortress, deliverer, strength, buckler, horn of salvation, and high tower. He recognizes the power of the Lord to help.

Verses 7 through 15 contain a vivid description of God's power and strength. The description makes me think of a mighty thunderstorm with the wind blowing and lightning flashing. What power is exhibited in that picture! Verses 16 through 19 show the victory that God, with all His power, brings in David's personal life.

Verse 27 through the end of the chapter continues to reveal the victory God gives David over his enemies. In verse 49, he gives thanks to the Lord for that victory. The Lord also gives us victories, but how many times do we forget to thank and praise Him for what He does?

What really catches my attention are the verses in the middle of the Psalm. In verses 20 and 24, David declares twice that

God rewarded or recompensed him according to one inward and one outward quality—his righteousness and the cleanness of his hands. If we want God to also work in our lives, we need to also have clean hands and be righteous. Are we walking in righteousness? Are our hands clean, or are we dabbling with our hands and dirtying them in the pleasures or sins of this world?

Between David's two declarations in verses 20 and 24, we have three verses that reveal how David had this righteous and clean life. In verse 21, he testifies, *"I have kept the ways of the LORD."* Are we doing His will and walking in His ways, offering ourselves as living sacrifices to the Lord as the first two verses of Romans 12 admonishes us?

Verse 22 shows us how David did this. *"For all his judgments were before me, and I did not put away his statutes from me."* His judgments are found in the Bible. Are we keeping His Word continually before us, reading and studying it? Are we memorizing it so we never have to "put it away" from us—even when we do not have a written copy with us?

David sought God's will for his life and made the Word of God part of his life. David also mentions staying away from sin in verse 23: *"I was also upright before him, and I kept myself from mine iniquity."* Do we stay as far away from sin as we can, or do we see how close we can get to the world and its attractions without actually sinning?

We have the same God David had. If we will walk with Him as David did, He will also give us the victory! Let's seek His will, stay in the Word, and stay away from sin. Victory can be ours!

# ℘salm 19

**I** BELIEVE VERSE one is beautiful: *"The heavens declare the glory of God; and the firmament sheweth his handywork."* Through verse six the Psalm continues to talk about the glory of God's creation. God declares His glory to anyone who will open his eyes and look!

But God does not stop with revealing Himself in creation; He then reveals Himself through His written Word so we can possess a more intimate relationship with Him. In verses seven and eight, four nouns and their adjectives describe His written Word: His perfect law, a sure testimony, right statutes, and pure commandments. These descriptions produce four results in our lives.

1) His perfect Law converts the soul (v. 7). His Word tells us how Christ came and died for our sins, so that by trusting only in Him we can have our sins forgiven.

2) His sure testimony makes wise the simple (v. 7). If we want wisdom, seeking it in God's Word will help us more than the philosophies of ungodly people.

3) His right statutes rejoice the heart (v. 8). So many people

today are seeking happiness by pursuing it. Real joy comes by studying God's principles in His Word and then following them. He tells us to love God first and then others. Serving Him and doing good to others will rejoice our heart.

4) His pure commandments enlighten the eyes (v. 8). Are you sometimes confused or not know where to turn or what to do in a situation? Bask in His Word for enlightenment.

In verse ten I love how God compares His Word to gold, reminding us that it is more desirable than gold. We can desire gold in the form of jewelry or money, and nothing is wrong with either of those—as long as we desire God and His Word more! But how many times does our world revolve around material things?

His Word is also sweeter than honey. I love sweets! I suppose that I like chocolate better than honey, but the comparison is still there. How sweet is the Word of God to me? Do I fill myself with it like I enjoy filling myself with chocolate? Or is it often on a back shelf as I give preference to other pursuits?

Verse 11 says that God's Word warns us, and when we do what it says, we will have great reward. How we need to keep His Word in an important place in our lives. We also need to do what the psalmist did at the end of the chapter: pray for cleansing. God's Word will show us where we need to "clean up." Let's pattern our prayers after verse 14, which says, *"Let the words of my mouth, and the meditation of my heart, be acceptable in thy sight, O LORD, my strength, and my redeemer."*

# Psalm 20

IN THE first four verses of this Psalm, David is praying for someone, asking God to hear, help, and bless them. What a reminder his words are that we need to pray for others! So many times our prayers are filled with the "gimmes"—gimme this and gimme that. Nothing is wrong with asking God to bless us and supply our needs, but I am afraid that too many of our prayers are centered around *me*. We need to take our eyes off of ourselves sometimes, notice the needs of others, and genuinely pray for them and their needs.

I keep and use a prayer notebook. One section contains a list of names of those for whom I pray every day—mostly family and close friends. I think of this list as praying for me and mine. Then I have a section where I enter requests from people who have asked for prayer. I put the date I started praying and then add the date it is answered. Some of these requests are answered quickly; some stay on the list for a long time. For me, having a record of how God has answered prayers and being reminded daily to pray for others is helpful.

But I do recognize that we need to pray for ourselves also. I love verse seven of this Psalm, which says, *"Some trust in chariots, and some in horses: but we will remember the name of the LORD our God."* We no longer use horses and chariots in battle, but in David's time, the armies relied on them. This verse has the idea of relying on our own resources, and so often we do that in our own lives. I know I do it far too much. What we need to do is remember the name of our God. We do that by calling to Him in prayer and depending on His strength to uphold us.

If we follow the admonition of this verse, the result is found in verse eight: *"They are brought down and fallen: but we are risen, and stand upright."* Our adversaries (the world, the flesh, and the Devil) will be defeated, and we will be victorious.

Let's pray for others and for victory in our lives. Let's also remember the name of the Lord our God daily.

# ℘salm 21

THIS PSALM mentions that the king has joy (or rejoices) in the strength of the Lord and His salvation. We may not be kings, but as Christians we are children of the King of kings, and even if we are the humblest of the humble here on the earth, we all have access to the Lord's strength and His salvation!

His salvation, of course, guarantees our home in heaven one day in the mansions He is preparing us—accommodations fit for a princess! Then, until we inhabit our heavenly home, we have His strength to meet the trials and difficulties we may face during our journey here on this earth. How we should rejoice in this knowledge!

The first half of the Psalm talks about God's blessing on the king, and then verse seven says, *"For the king trusteth in the LORD, and through the mercy of the most High he shall not be moved."* Although the king had the highest position possible, He knew He needed to trust in Someone higher than himself. We also need to remember where our trust should be—not in ourselves, but in the Lord Who is most High. How often do we think that our position or possessions come because of what we have done in our strength, rather than as blessings from a merciful God Who loves us in spite of ourselves!

The following verses share how God gave victory over the king's enemies. The king knew that victory was not because of his own strength or power. Verse 13 says, *"Be thou exalted, LORD, in thine own strength: so will we sing and praise thy power."*

So many times we do one of two things when the Enemy attacks—give up or try to win in our own strength. Either way, we are forgetting that the strength of the Lord—not what we can do in our own strength—gives us the victory. Let's remember to trust in Him and then remember to give Him the honor and praise for what He does.

# $\mathfrak{P}$salm 22

IN MANY Psalms, David started with a negative situation and then ended with praising God for His goodness, mercy, or deliverance. Although David stated his suffering and persecution in the beginning of this Psalm, he remembers in verse five how God had delivered Israel in the past. *"They cried unto thee, and were delivered: they trusted in thee, and were not confounded."*

Finally, in verse 22 He changes focus. *"I will declare thy name unto my brethren: in the midst of the congregation will I praise thee."* In the next verses he tells those who fear the Lord to praise Him because He remembers our afflictions. Verse 24 ends, *"When He cried unto Him, He heard."* God always knows our difficulties and hears our cries, even if the answer does not seem evident. The psalmist continues, *"My praise shall be of thee in the great congregation: I will pay my vows before them that fear him"* (v. 25).

He continues to praise God and promises to keep his vows. We are not to bargain with God, saying, "If You help me, I will do such and such." I think the vow we should always have in our hearts is to obey Him.

So, I see three lessons to practice in times of difficulties, trials, or persecution:

1) Remember how God answered and helped in the PAST.

2) Praise God in the PRESENT—even if you don't see deliverance yet.

3) Continue to praise God in the FUTURE and decide to always obey His Word.

Let's always remember God hears us, let's believe He will answer, and let's praise Him when the answer comes.

# ℑ℘salm 23

Psalm 23 is a very familiar Psalm to most of us. I also believe we often recite it without thinking what it means or how the passage applies to us. A sheep is a fairly helpless creature and cannot care for itself. Like every sheep needs a shepherd, we also need guidance. When we trust the Lord as our Saviour, then we have the Lord Himself as our guide and help.

Verse one says, *"I shall not want."* We live in a "gimme, gimme" society—always wanting something more or better. But the *want* in this verse does not mean desire, but need. The Lord will provide our needs, not necessarily our desires.

Human beings are made up of body, soul, and spirit. This Psalm mentions how our Shepherd helps in these three areas. Verse two says He provides food and drink—our physical needs. For a time while my husband and I were in Bible college, we ate only rice, but we did not starve! Once all we had for a Sunday dinner was oatmeal. Although we do not live on T-bone steaks now, we do eat well. But those times in college remain precious memories of watching our Shepherd provide.

Verse three reminds us that He restores our soul. He gives

us emotional strength and healing when we are frustrated or stressed out—and who does not get stressed out at times in this fast-paced world? Then He leads us in righteousness. If we follow Him, that path will give added rest to our soul. We will avoid the pitfalls and negative effects that walking in the world brings.

Verse four says He helps us spiritually. We need not fear in the face of death if He is our Saviour and Shepherd. The psalmist also says, *"I will fear no evil: for thou art with me"* (v. 4). We don't need to fear any of Satan's evil attacks when we are walking with our Shepherd. And in verse six, the psalmist gives the following assurance: *"I will dwell in the house of the LORD forever."* We may pass through some hard times or difficulties here, but we have the promise of a perfect place where we will spend all of eternity. It can't get better than that.

Let's follow our Shepherd, trusting Him to guide us and give us everything we need in this life. Let's also rejoice in the fact that we have a future home in heaven forever with Him.

# Psalm 24

VERSE THREE asks who will stand in God's holy place, and the answer found in verse 4 is twofold: clean hands and a pure heart. This response reflects on both the external and the internal.

*"Clean hands"* does not refer to washing our hands before meals! Rather, the verse is talking about the things we do that others can observe—in other words being pure and right in our doings. Are we pure and honest in our dealings with others? Do we try to live by God's commandments and the principles in His Word?

In contrast, *"a pure heart"* refers more to our inner being—our thoughts and attitudes that cannot be visibly seen. These thoughts and attitudes are often reflected in our actions. Two examples are cited in verse four: vanity and deceitful swearing.

*Vanity* means "being too proud of and interested in yourself," which to me would indicate self-centeredness. A vain person thinks only of himself and wants his desires fulfilled, rather than his having a genuine interest in others and a desire to help meet their needs.

Deceitful swearing could refer to profane or crude speech, but I think of it as being more than that. If we "swear" or promise and say we will do something and then don't do it, we are deceiving others. Do we strive to keep our promises? Can people depend on us if we say we will do something? They should be able to do so.

If we have clean hands and a pure heart and avoid vanity and deceitfulness, God promises in verse 5 that we will receive blessings from Him: *"He shall receive the blessing from the LORD."* Let's seek those blessings!

# 𝔓salm 25

𝖁ERSE eight tells us, *"Good and upright is the LORD."* God is good, and God is upright or righteous.

We finish every service of our church quoting: "God is good all the time; all the time God is good." And He certainly is! He is good even when some circumstances or situations in our lives do not seem to be good.

My husband sometimes preaches on Romans 8:28, *"And we know that all things work together for good to them that love God."* He illustrates this verse with the example of making a cake. No one likes to eat flour, raw eggs, or baking powder by themselves, but they are necessary ingredients for a cake. When added to the tasty ingredients of milk and sugar, the result is a delicious cake. All of the ingredients are necessary, and when combined and baked, they produce a desirable product. In the same way, what may seem bad to us is as necessary as all of what seems good, and God says they all work together for our good if we love Him.

God is also upright, or righteous, and His desire is for us to live righteously too. In verses 8 through 12, almost immediately after using the term *upright*, the passage addresses three groups of people whom God teaches.

The first is *"sinners."* We all are born sinners, and before we can please God, we must be cleansed of our sins by accepting the Lord as our Saviour.

The next group He teaches are the *"meek."* The word *meek* can mean "gentle, kind, or yielding." Once we accept God's gift of eternal life, we should want to follow Him and yield to His will. He teaches us how through the Bible.

Verse 12 says that God teaches those who *"fear him."* That *fear* does not mean being afraid of God, but having awe and respect for Him. God will teach such a man to walk *"in the way that he shall choose"* (v. 12b). God will guide us in the best path as we follow Him.

Let's allow God to teach us in these ways and claim the promise in verse 13: *"His soul shall dwell at ease; and his seed shall inherit the earth."* God will bless us, and He will also bless our children.

# Psalm 26

In verse one, the psalmist says that he walked in his integrity and trusted in the Lord; and therefore, he would not slide. Have you ever slipped on something wet or icy? When I was expecting our first son, we lived in an upstairs apartment with outside stairs. One morning I needed to go out, and I did not anticipate how icy the stairs were. I slipped, landing on the part of my anatomy that I normally sit on as I bounced down the remainder of the steps. I was between four to five months into my pregnancy, so I scheduled an ultrasound, and everything was fine except for a few bruises. My trust in myself had been sadly misplaced! But when we trust in the Lord, our spiritual steps are secure.

In verse three, the psalmist said he had walked in God's truth. How can we do that? We need to stay grounded in His Word, the Bible. The psalmist also mentioned several types of people with whom he did not keep company: vain persons, dissemblers, evildoers, and the wicked. Of course, we need to be kind to everyone, but we should not choose these types of people as close friends or constant companions.

In verse 11, the psalmist again addresses walking in his integrity. *Integrity* means "being honest and having strong moral principles." As well as avoiding the wrong kind of company, we need to seek to follow the principles we find in God's Word.

If we do that, we will be able to say as the psalmist in verse 12: *"My foot standeth in an even place...."* As I get older, I try to be careful of where I step to avoid falling. I have seen too many people break bones because of a simple fall! I pay attention especially to places that are not level or even—such as stairs or near curbs. Even being careful, I have fallen flat several times at curbs or because of other obstructions in the sidewalk. I had sore and scraped hands and knees, but thankfully no broken bones! But how much better it is to have an even place to walk. When we walk following God's principles, we are walking on even ground.

Let's walk in our integrity.

# $\mathfrak{P}$salm 27

I n verse one of this Psalm, the writer calls the Lord his light, his salvation, and his strength. Because of all that God is in the psalmist's life, he does not need to be afraid.

When God is our salvation—when we have trusted Him as our personal Saviour—we do not need to fear eternity. Romans 6:23b says the *"gift of God is eternal life through Jesus Christ our Lord."* If we have asked Him to forgive our sins and trusted in Him alone, our eternal destiny is secure.

God is also our light. A light reveals the path and illumines the way. As we walk with God and follow Him, we do not need to fear the future. He will guide us along the way no matter what comes across our path. We may not be able to see far ahead, but we need only enough light to see the next step.

The Lord is also our strength. We do not need to fear the battles or difficulties in our lives because we do not need to depend on ourselves. In fact, trying to do so is a guarantee of failure. Philippians 4:13 says, *"I can do all things **through Christ** which strengtheneth me."*

The last verse of the Psalm contains a promise: *"Wait on the*

LORD: *be of good courage, and he shall strengthen thine heart: wait, I say, on the LORD.*" The secret to not being afraid, having courage, and being strengthened is to wait on the Lord. In this verse, God twice instructs us to wait on the Lord.

*Wait* means to "allow time to pass until something happens." We expect God to do something, so we look for His hand in resolving our situation. But the fact that we have to allow time to pass can be frustrating, especially in today's fast-moving world. Everyone wants immediate gratification, immediate answers. But our timetable usually is not the same as God's. We need to wait for Him to act in His time.

Waiting patiently is not easy, but when we do, He promises His strength. Let's wait on the Lord.

# $\mathcal{P}$salm 28

HAVE YOU ever felt like you do not know where to turn for help? Perhaps every person has been there at one point or another. We sometimes look everywhere except to the only source that always has the answer—the Lord. But the psalmist knew exactly where to turn. He cried to the Lord because he knew the Lord was his rock.

Many slums in Brazil are precariously built on the sides of hills. During heavy rains, mud slides often occur, and the houses are washed down the hill and destroyed. These slums are ruined because they were not built upon a solid foundation—upon rock!

If we do not build our life on our Rock, the Lord Jesus Christ, and His principles, our life can be ruined. Our dreams and hopes will be washed away in the storms of life. If we cry and our Rock is silent, we will become like the psalmist who says, *"I become like them that go down into the pit"* (v. 1b).

We hear about people who are in the pit of depression, which is exactly what this verse makes me think of. Anxiety and depression have become undeniable problems in today's world. Too many people depend on antidepressants and sleep aids to get them through their days and nights. I am not saying there is never a need for medication, but much of it could be avoided if we learned how to cry out to our Rock to resolve our problems, concerns, and difficulties.

He is always ready to hear us if we will call on Him. In verse six, the psalmist says, *"Blessed be the LORD, because He hath heard the voice of my supplications."* The psalmist knew where to turn, and he also remembered to be thankful and to bless the Lord for answering.

Verse seven continues, *"my heart trusted in him, and I am helped: therefore my heart greatly rejoiceth; and with my song will I praise him."* If we turn to Him and trust Him, we will be helped as the psalmist was helped. And if we rejoice in that help, we will be brought out of our pit. Let's cry to Him out of our pit, and then let's rejoice and sing His praises when He delivers us!

# 𝔓salm 29

ERSE TWO of this Psalm says, *"Give unto the LORD the glory due unto his name...."* His name is above all names. We could go on and on citing the many names attributed to the Lord throughout the Bible. Just the names given to Him in Isaiah 9:6, which include, *"Wonderful, Counsellor, The mighty God, The everlasting Father, The Prince of Peace,"* are an awesome description of our Lord—and these five are only the beginning of the list of God's names.

Verses throughout the rest of this Psalm mention the voice of the Lord and its overwhelming power. These verses make me think about the creation. God used only His voice to create our world in all its wonder and intricacy! I will never understand how someone can believe in evolution, especially after seeing the incredible complexity of creation. Science discovers more and more that this complexity is only compounded. To think that God spoke it all into existence! What a mighty God!

But in all His might and greatness, He cares for us individually. The psalmist says in verse 11, *"The LORD will give strength unto his people; the LORD will bless his people with peace."*

This verse spotlights two areas of His interest for us. First, as seen in other Psalms, God imparts strength. He wants to give power for us to have victory in our lives. He cares about our struggles.

He also blesses us with peace. Wars and turmoil will always be present in this world, but in the midst of it all, we can have personal peace in our lives.

We receive peace with God when we accept what Christ did for us on the cross, ask forgiveness for our sins, and receive Him as our Saviour. But there is so much more. He gives us peace in the midst of problems as we give Him glory with our lives and walk in His ways.

Let's *"give unto the LORD the glory due unto His name"* every day in our lives.

# Psalm 30

*I*LOVE THE promise in the second part of verse five: *"weeping may endure for a night, but joy cometh in the morning."* God never said the Christian life would be a bed of roses. We live in a world with ups and downs, with weeping but also laughing, with sorrows but also joys. But how did the psalmist turn his weeping to joy?

Verse 8 says, *"I cried to thee, O LORD; and unto the LORD I made supplication."* Too often when problems, difficulties, or hard times come, we tend to mope, be sad, and hold a pity party for ourselves. We turn our thoughts inward instead of upward, as the psalmist did.

We might ask, "Why did this happen to me?" That question is not wrong if we are analyzing the situation to see what we can do to resolve the situation or avoid a similar one in the future. But asking with the attitude that we did not deserve to be in such a situation or that we deserve something better is wrong. We need to accept any situation God puts us in, knowing that the difficult time will come to an end.

The psalmist confirms this fact in verse 11 when he states

that God changed his mourning to dancing and clothed him with gladness instead of sackcloth, which is a sign of mourning.

The psalmist called on the Lord in his time of sadness, and God answered. In verse 12 the psalmist states that the end of his story was *"that my glory may sing praise to thee, and not be silent."* How often do we pray to God and when He answers we forget to thank Him, or we thank Him in our hearts but do not praise Him audibly. In everything, God should get the glory, so let's especially remember to praise Him when our weeping turns to joy.

Let's be like the psalmist, who concludes this Psalm with the words, *"O Lord my God, I will give thanks unto thee for ever."*

# Psalm 31

VERSE 12 OF this Psalm opens with an interesting statement: *"I am forgotten as a dead man out of mind."* Have you ever thought you may as well be dead for as little as people pay attention to you or seem to care about you? Or maybe you feel like the second part of that verse, which says, *"I am like a broken vessel."* Perhaps you feel like you do not know where to turn to fix the brokenness of your life. Or maybe your spirit is broken and you are depressed or despondent.

The psalmist had similar feelings, but thankfully he knew exactly how to resolve his problems. Verse 14 starts with the transformational word "BUT"—*"But I trusted in thee, O LORD...."* The psalmist knew that the Lord was the One Who could fix his negative feelings and his brokenness. Likewise, He can do the same for us.

The psalmist completed verse 14 by saying, *"Thou art my God."* He did not simply say, "Thou art God." He personalized the statement with "my." Many people believe in God, but they do not know Him personally. We need to know Him as our Saviour and as the Lord of our lives. But even those who know

Him as Saviour forget that He desires to have a personal walk with us. He wants us to feel Him in our lives daily as He helps us with our needs.

But even as the psalmist acknowledged his trust in God, he falters yet again and says, *"I am cut off from before thine eyes."* Each of us tends to ride this revolving cycle at some time. We are depressed or discouraged because our eyes are not on God. Then we turn to Him and acknowledge our trust in Him. But soon we are discouraged again and think God is not seeing us.

Thankfully, the psalmist realizes His need and acknowledges, *"nevertheless thou heardest the voice of my supplications when I cried unto thee"* (v. 22b). The Lord is always there to hear our cry and heal our brokenness when we call on Him. Let's take heart in the words of the psalmist in verse 24: *"Be of good courage, and he shall strengthen your heart, all ye that hope in the Lord."*

# $\mathfrak{P}$salm 32

$I$N CORRIE ten Boom's book *The Hiding Place,* she tells how her family was able to hide and protect many Jewish people in a narrow hidden room they had constructed. In verse 7 the psalmist states that God is his hiding place. He continues, *"Thou shalt preserve me from trouble."*

When God is hiding us, He preserves us from trouble. That promise does not mean we will never have troubles, but God will protect us from their destructive effects on our life. That same verse concludes, *"thou shalt compass me about with songs of deliverance."* When trouble came, the psalmist was delivered. How can we receive that same deliverance?

The very next verse says that God will instruct and teach us in the way we should go. He teaches us through His Word. If we will study His Word and follow its principles, we will know the way we should go and be preserved from trouble—just as the Jews in the ten Boom's hidden room were preserved from the enemy, even as they searched the house.

Verse 9 warns us not to be like a horse or a mule that needs a snaffle bit in its mouth to be controlled. We need to willingly allow God to guide us.

This Psalm says that God will guide us with His eye (v. 8). Have you ever gotten "that look" from one of your parents? You knew right away what they wanted you to do or not to do! And you knew your life would be much happier if you paid attention and acquiesced to that look.

Even so, we are much happier when we allow God's eye to guide us. We don't want to be like a horse or a mule with no understanding. Let's be led willingly by God's eye, rather than forcefully by a bit like a horse. In doing so, we can, as verse 11 says, be glad, rejoice, and shout for joy.

# ℘salm 33

T HE WORD *comely* in verse one makes me think of the desire to look attractive or beautiful. Women especially like
to fix themselves up, spending time to do their hair or put on
makeup. We like to look nice for others.

But the word *comely* has a broader meaning of "agreeable"
or "suitable." I believe this meaning is more appropriate for
*comely* in verse one. Praise is a suitable and agreeable charac-
teristic of the righteous or upright person. I can picture God's
looking down and smiling from heaven as we praise Him and
then thinking of us as comely.

We should praise God for many reasons. Verse five tells us
that the earth is full of the goodness of God. The next verses
describe how He formed His creation simply by speaking a
word, which shows how powerful our God is. And when we
see how majestic His creation is, we have even more reason to
praise His works.

Verse eight says to stand in awe of the Lord. I picture myself standing with my mouth wide open, admiring and being
astonished at the beauty and majesty of God's creation. We

certainly should praise Him for the beautiful world He has made.

After revealing His might in nature, the rest of the chapter shows us His might in caring for and protecting His people. Verse 16 tells us a king will not be saved by a mighty army nor a mighty man by his strength. God is mightier than both. He can save us from any problem that arises in our life.

Verse 17 talks about the strength of a horse, which was important in the days of the psalmist. But that great strength is also useless for deliverance. God is greater than all the strength of every horse combined.

Verse 20 sums up the entire Psalm: *"Our soul waiteth for the Lord: he is our help and our shield."* The God Who formed and controls all creation—both nature and man—is our help in difficulties and our shield from the Enemy.

Let's be comely in our praise of Him and say as the psalmist in verse 21, *"For our heart shall rejoice in him, because we have trusted in his holy name."*

# Psalm 34

IN BOTH verse four and verse six, the psalmist sought or cried
to the Lord, and the Lord heard him. In verse four, he was
delivered from his fears. Our fears can be very strong. Whether
we have fear of tangible things or of situations that might never
come to pass, fear is very real. But if we call on the Lord, He can
deliver us from our fears. If we remember that the Lord is in control and loves us, we can calm our fears concerning matters that
are completely out of our hands and might not even happen!

In verse six the psalmist is delivered from His troubles because He called on God. We all have problems and difficulties
at times, but when we turn to the Lord, we can trust that He
will resolve the problem in His way and in His timing.

Verse seven says, *"The angel of the LORD encampeth round
about them that fear him, and delivereth them."* This verse makes
me think of the story of Elijah's servant, who was allowed to see
a huge army surrounding Elijah and his servant with no seeming way of escape. Elijah asked God to open his servant's eyes,
and he then saw a fiery army of the Lord in the skies around
them. The enemy was vastly outnumbered.

Our Enemy is also outnumbered. We just have to see or believe with the eyes of faith. God will give the victory.

Verse 18 tells us the Lord will be with us and save us in two situations. The psalmist first mentions times when we have a broken heart. We all have or will pass through times when our hearts are broken. People will disappoint us, or we will experience the loss of loved ones. But God promises to be near.

He also mentions a contrite spirit. *Contrite* means "remorseful" or "repentant." First He saves us when we come to Him in repentance, asking forgiveness of our sins. But once we are saved, we will still sometimes do wrong. Anytime we are repentant, He forgives us yet again—not to give us salvation for that is a one-time forever gift. But He restores our fellowship with Him.

Verse 19 tells us we will have many afflictions, but we are again reminded that the Lord delivers us from them all. Over and over in this Psalm, we are told that God delivers us. Let's remind ourselves of that promise every day and trust in God's deliverance.

# Psalm 35

WHEN SOMEONE is treated unfairly or suffers unjustly, it is easy to get upset and to wonder why God would allow such injustice. But even when it does not seem like God is in control, He is. Justice will be served in the end—it just may not be in our timing. It may not even be in this lifetime, but God will serve justice.

In this Psalm, the psalmist asks God to plead his cause. *"For without cause have they hid for me their net in a pit"* (v. 7). Verse 11 says, *"False witnesses did rise up..."* and verse 12 reveals why he needed God to plead his cause: *"They rewarded me evil for good."* According to these passages, the psalmist certainly was being treated unjustly, and he begs God to judge his enemies.

But even in the midst of his troubles and his desire to be delivered, he states that when his enemy was sick, he fasted and prayed for him. *"I behaved myself as though he had been my friend or brother..."* (v. 14).

We live in an unjust and sinful world. What happened to the psalmist will also happen to us. The world does not treat righteous people kindly. When we try to live for the Lord, those who do not love the Lord will often seek to be unkind or even seek our hurt.

God tells us to love our enemies, which is not an easy task. But the psalmist is a great example to us. Can we say we do good to those who treat us wrongly? We should be able to.

At the close of the Psalm, the psalmist says, *"Let the LORD be magnified, which hath pleasure in the prosperity of his servant. And my tongue shall speak of thy righteousness and of thy praise all the day long"* (vv. 27b, 28).

Let's allow God to be judge in His time. May we constantly praise and magnify Him for His goodness and care.

# Psalm 36

THIS PSALM begins by talking about the *transgression* or sin of the wicked. Verse 3 lists two characteristics that describe the wicked man and then two qualities that are absent from His life.

The two attributes mentioned pertain to his words. Our spoken words come as a result of our thoughts and then spill over into our actions. One act leads to another. We think something, we speak, and then we act. The two words describing the wicked are *iniquity* (sin) and *deceit*.

Sinful thoughts or words would be the opposite of the type of thoughts the Bible tells us to have. Philippians 4:8 tells us our thoughts should be true, honest, just, pure, lovely, and of good report. We should not fill our heads and mouths with sinful words as the wicked do.

Have you ever said something unkind about someone, only to try to justify your words by saying it was true? What we say should always be true, but we do not have to share everything we know simply because it is true. Let's test all that we think or say within the confines of Philippians 4:8:

- Is it true?
- Is it honest?
- Is it just?
- Is it pure?
- Is it lovely?
- Is it a good report?

If not, let's keep the matter to ourselves.

We should not want our mouths full of iniquity like the wicked. Neither should we not want our mouths full of deceit. Have you ever told a "little white lie" perhaps to avoid trouble? A lie is a lie, and when we tell one, we are filling our mouths with deceit. Let's not follow the path of the wicked.

The two qualities absent from the wicked are found in the second part of verse three, which says, *"he hath left off to be wise, and to do good."* The word *wise* means "to show experience, knowledge, and good judgment." Proverbs 1:7 says, *"The fear of the LORD is the beginning of knowledge: but fools despise wisdom and instruction."* The wicked have no fear of God, so how are they to obtain knowledge and wisdom? The wicked have also left off doing good. Verse 4 tells us they do not hate evil. In other words, they have substituted evil for good.

Let's run from the example of the wicked—from their sinful and deceitful ways. Let's be wise and do good.

# Psalm 37

HAVE YOU ever thought that often people who do not love God and perhaps live their lives without any concern for the Christian principles of honesty, love, and respect seem to have perfect lives? They often have new cars, good jobs, beautiful houses, and expensive clothes. This Psalm tells us not to fret or be envious of them because they will be cut down and wither as the grass.

They may keep their earthly goods for what seems a long time, but at the end of this life, they will have nothing. If we are trying to serve God, we are storing up our riches in heaven, where we will enjoy them for all eternity. Verse 16 reminds us, *"A little that a righteous man hath is better than the riches of many wicked."*

Instead of focusing on the riches of this world, verses three through five tell us three things we should do.

1) *"Trust in the LORD, and do good."* Verse three says that in doing so, we will dwell in the land and be fed. God will supply our needs if we will take our eyes off ourselves and do good to others.

2) Verse four instructs us to, *"Delight thyself also in the LORD; and he shall give thee the desires of thine heart."* I believe many people view this verse as a blank check to get anything they want from God. In a sense this is true, but if we are meeting the condition of delighting in Him, our delights will not be a new car or a huge, beautiful house. Our desires will be what glorifies Him in our lives.

3) Verse five continues, *"Commit thy way unto the LORD; trust also in Him, and He shall bring it to pass."* What will He bring to pass? I believe this refers to the desires of our heart, mentioned in the previous verse. But these desires have been tweaked because we have delighted in Him. I think we will want whatever God thinks is best for us. And because we want what God wants, the very next verse says He will bring forth our righteousness as the light.

May our lives reflect His righteousness. Let's be a light in this world for Him.

# Psalm 38

FROM THE very beginning of this chapter, the psalmist declares how broken and miserable He is. *"For mine iniquities are gone over mine head: as an heavy burden they are too heavy for me"* (v. 4).

In verse five, the psalmist addresses his foolishness, and in verse eight, he says he is feeble and sore broken. I can identify with Him! At times I have felt like the worst mother, or wife, or Christian, or missionary, or all of the above at the same time! We can become bogged down because of sin—even if it is "only" a sin of omission, like neglecting our Bible reading or prayer. Or we can be troubled over the consequences of our foolishness—something we did or said without really thinking it through first. These situations can become overwhelming and cause us great *mourning, disquiet,* or *failed strength*—to name a few of the terms the psalmist uses in referring to the troubles in his life.

But the psalmist comes to his senses in verse 15 when he says, *"For in thee, O LORD, do I hope: thou wilt hear, O Lord my God."* He knew where to turn, and he knew the Lord would be there for him. But merely hoping in the Lord and knowing He will answer is not enough. We have to act further upon that knowledge.

According to verse 18, the psalmist acted. *"For I will declare mine iniquity; I will be sorry for my sin."* We need to be sorry for our sins, not only of commission but also of omission. We should not simply be sorry that we are in a situation that makes us despondent.

Too many people are sorry they got themselves in a mess. Now they want out of that mess, but they do not want to repent of the wrong they did that put them there. They are not willing to confess and turn from the sin in their life.

Let us be like the psalmist and be sorry for our sins. Let's confess them to the Lord. Then He can forgive and bless our lives.

# Psalm 39

OUR TONGUE is difficult to control. Some people who "fly off the handle" often excuse themselves, saying, "This is the way God made me." They believe that this defense will cover the trauma they have caused with their tongue. Some people say, "I just tell it like it is." God made us with different personality traits, but that God-made difference does not mean we should not try to improve in areas of our life that need some work. Neither of these excuses will exempt us from a problem of anger.

The psalmist describes a familiar scene in the first three verses. He says he will keep quiet. He plans not to say anything—either bad or good. He holds his peace until matters begin to smolder inside of Him, then accelerated. When the fire burned within him, he finally spoke his piece! As a follow-up in verse four, he admitted his frailty. We, like the psalmist, are also weak when it comes to taming our tongue.

Along with anger, another problem that arises with our tongue is gossip. A story is told of a woman who constantly gossiped and one day confessed this penchant to the pastor. He told her to get a feather pillow and throw the feathers into the wind. Then He told her to gather all of the feathers back into the pillow. When she said that was not possible, he reminded her that neither could she retract her words of gossip. Once spoken, the harm was done.

Our undisciplined tongues can do much harm—whether we use them in anger or in gossip. The psalmist admits in verse five, *"verily every man at His best state is altogether vanity."* But he knew where the answer was, and in verse seven, he says his hope is in the Lord.

Whether our problem is controlling our tongue or any other sin or weakness in our lives, our hope is also in the Lord. Let's declare as the psalmist did: *"Deliver me from all my transgressions..."* (v. 8).

# ℌsalm 40

THIS PSALM'S opening verse begins with the psalmist crying to the Lord. Several facts present themselves in verses two and three. First, God delivered him from a horrible pit. In other words, the psalmist considered himself a terrible sinner. In all actuality, we all should see ourselves in this way. But no matter what we have done, God loves us and wants to deliver us. Whether we have so-called "big" sins or "little" sins, our righteousness is nothing compared to the holiness of God. But He still hears our cry and will deliver each of us as He did the psalmist.

Second, God set the feet of the psalmist on a rock. Without God, our lives will forever flounder on shifting sand. If you undertake the building of a house, that house will need to be built on a firm foundation. Jesus told the parable of the two men who built houses—one built on a rock, and one built on the sand. When the storms came, the house on the sand fell, but the one on the rock stood firm. Jesus is our Rock, and because of Him, we have our life sitting on a firm foundation.

Third, God established the psalmist's goings. Only if our

lives are built on Him can we stand firm even when the storms of life come. Each step will be on firm ground because God is directing our lives. If we follow His lead, our steps will be sure, and we will not falter or fall.

Unfortunately, we do not always continue following God's lead. Several verses showcase how the psalmist did God's will and preached righteousness, but then verse 12 says, *"mine iniquities have taken hold upon me, so that I am not able to look up; they are more than the hairs of mine head: therefore my heart faileth me."* I don't know how many hairs the psalmist had on his head, but the point is that he had many sins. We can also allow sins to control our lives again—if we stop following God's established way for us.

Thankfully, the psalmist knew what to do. Verse 13 says, *"Be pleased, O LORD, to deliver me: O LORD, make haste to help me."* God will always hear and restore our communion with Him when we call out to Him. He loves us unconditionally, so He is always ready to help.

Let's always remember the truth of verse 17, which says, *"But I am poor and needy; yet the LORD thinketh upon me: thou art my help and my deliverer; make no tarrying, O my God."* Let's call upon Him for help when we have sin in our life.

# ℘salm 41

Have you ever felt poor? During a short time when my husband was in seminary, we were very short on money. We somehow managed to scrape up enough to buy a bag of rice, and we had rice for all of our meals—cooked, fried, or in whatever novel way I could think of to have variety. Then we would scrape up enough for another bag—just rice—nothing else.

Then there was a period of time that we went without a car because we could not afford one. We were already in Brazil as missionaries, and thankfully we were in a somewhat small town with reliable public transportation. We either walked a half hour to church or took the bus.

We had some needs, but I never considered us "poor"—at least not in comparison to others who really had nothing. But during those times, we had people who gave us a helping hand.

On the other side of the coin, when we know of someone with needs and we have the means to give, we like to help. Many beg because they simply don't want to work, so I try to be careful, but verse one of this Psalm says, *"Blessed is he that considereth the poor: the LORD will deliver him in time of trouble."*

We need to open our eyes and notice those around us who might have a need, whether it be food, clothing, or money to pay a bill. When we are conscious of the needs of others, the Lord promises to help in time of trouble.

But He also promises to do more. Verse two says He will preserve us and keep us alive. I don't want to die before I have to because I failed to care for the less fortunate! Verse two also says we will be blessed, and we will not be delivered to our enemies. Do you want God's blessing? Be considerate of the poor.

Verse three mentions that God will strengthen us when we are sick if we help the poor. We should not give so that we can receive; rather, we need to have a genuine concern for helping the poor in order to reap God's blessings on us.

# ℑsalm 42

I LOVE THE picture painted in the very first verse of this Psalm: *"As the hart panteth after the water brooks, so panteth my soul after thee, O God."* The hart is an exquisitely graceful animal that can run like the wind. The word *pant* means "a quick, short breath, usually from exertion or excitement." In my mind's eyes, I can see a thirsty deer standing beside a gentle flowing brook, excited to get a drink from the rippling water.

In the same way, the psalmist is excited about having his spiritual thirst satisfied by the Lord, especially after having been troubled and depressed. Three times in this Psalm, he mentions being cast down and disquieted (vv. 5, 6, 11).

He includes another allusion to water in verse seven. In this Scripture, he pictures a near drowning- *"all thy waves and thy billows are gone over me."* Sometimes in the difficulties of life, we can feel like we are drowning in our problems! And we might momentarily, like the psalmist did (v. 9), think God has forgotten us. He has not forgotten; sometimes we simply cannot see Him with the deep waters around us.

But twice in this Psalm, when the psalmist talked about

being cast down, He said He would hope in God and praise Him (vv. 5, 11).

Let's do the same! Let's hope in God, and He will lift us out of the deep waters and put us beside the calm brook. Then we can excitedly drink from His calm waters and praise Him for what He has done.

# Psalm 43

H AVE YOU ever gotten up in total darkness and tripped or stubbed your toe because you didn't turn on the light? Once when I got up in the middle of the night, I began groping for the light switch in the dark and stepped barefoot on a live cockroach! I certainly wished I had found the light sooner!

In verse three the psalmist asked God to let His light and truth lead him. Psalm 119:105 says, *"Thy word is a lamp unto my feet and a light unto my path."* Verse 142 of Psalm 119 concludes, *"and thy law is the truth."* So where do we find light and truth to guide us? From God's Word!

The Bible will help us walk without tripping in our Christian life. To take full advantage of the leading of the Word of God, we need to do more than just read it. We need to study it, meditate on it, and memorize it so we have it with us in our heart all the time.

After asking for God's light and truth to lead him, the psalmist added, *"let them bring me unto thy holy hill, and to thy tabernacles."* He knew that, along with God's Word, being in the house of God is important. True, we can worship God out under the stars or sitting beside a beautiful lake, but we also need to be in His house. At church we can learn more of His Word from the studies and the preaching, as well as enjoy fellowshipping with other believers to strengthen our Christian lives.

Verse four reiterates the desire of the psalmist to praise God in His house. In prayer we can praise Him for what He has done, as well as make our petitions to Him.

In the five verses in this chapter, the psalmist outlines the three ingredients that are very important in helping Christians grow in their walk with God:

1) The Bible—light and truth

2) The church—His tabernacles

3) Prayer—praising Him

Let's include all three of these ingredients in our life to grow in the Lord.

# $\mathfrak{P}$salm 44

$\mathbf{D}$ID YOU ever ask your parents or grandparents or someone else older than you to tell you stories from when they were growing up? My great aunt was a missionary in Pakistan for 40 years. She would often share stories of when she was living there. I will never forget her telling about being careful to look in her shoes in the morning before putting them on to make sure a snake had not made one of them His bed during the night! Hearing stories from the past can be both fun and even instructional.

The psalmist tells of how they had heard stories from their fathers of what great things God had done for the nation of Israel *"in the times of old."* He asserted that they did not conquer the land on their own but because of God's hand. The psalmist did not trust in his bow or sword, but he trusted in God alone to save them from their enemies. And God did save them.

We should strive to be as the psalmist, trusting God because we remember what He did. As we look to the past to see how God has blessed, we can trust Him to be with us in the present and the future.

But then the psalmist tells how Israel was being defeated by the enemy and were being made into a reproach. Yet He said in verse 18, *"Our heart is not turned back; neither have our steps declined from thy way."*

At times, we may seem immersed in problems and difficulties. We saw how God blessed in the past and wonder why He is no longer blessing. Although we may not and do not need to understand, we should decide we will not turn aside. We should continue to faithfully serve God in the difficult times and in the times that we may wonder what He is doing.

The psalmist ends the Psalm by saying, *"Arise for our help, and redeem us for thy mercies' sake."* He trusted God would answer and help.

Like David, let's also call on God and believe He will hear us and answer.

# $\mathfrak{P}$salm 45

ERSE TWO, which is speaking of Jesus, says, *"therefore God has blessed thee for ever."* Verse three speaks of His glory and majesty, and the following verses speak of truth, meekness, and righteousness, and the fact that He will reign forever. What a glorious description of our wonderful Lord!

Verse nine makes mention of a queen, and verse eleven says, *"So shall the king greatly desire thy beauty...."* We women often think we are less than beautiful, and we tend to focus on our negative qualities. We don't like the color of our eyes or the shape of our nose or ears. If we have straight hair, we want it curly. If we have curly hair, we want it straight. We think we are too tall or too short. We think we are too fat or too thin. But God, our King, thinks we are beautiful—precisely the way we are. He created each of us exactly the way He wanted us. If we can improve some areas, nothing is wrong with working on those. However, we do need to accept ourselves the way God made us and realize we are beautiful in His sight.

Verse 11 continues saying, *"for he is thy LORD; and worship thou him."* When we begin to focus less on ourselves and more on the Lord Who created us and saved us, we will be more inclined to worship Him.

Let's realize God made us the way we are and loves us. Let's take the focus off ourselves and turn it to our Lord. Let's think about Him and worship Him for all of His glorious attributes.

# Psalm 46

Have you ever faced a natural disaster like an earthquake, tornado, hurricane, or tsunami? Thankfully, I am familiar with these only through pictures or videos on television or Facebook. The worst weather situations I have faced include heavy rain, snowstorms, or hail. I can only imagine how terrible experiencing a natural disaster would be. Yet the psalmist describes those types of situations in verses two and three and says He will not fear.

Why won't He be afraid? The answer is found in verse one, which says, *"God is our refuge and strength, a very present help in trouble."* A *refuge* is a place of safety. When I think of a refuge, I picture a storm cellar on a farm used in case of a tornado. To be protected, those seeking a place of safety and shelter must get into the cellar. We likewise need to come to Christ for salvation in order for God to be our refuge. He is also our strength, allowing us to withstand the storms of life and the attacks of our Enemy, Satan.

I love the words *"a very present help in trouble."* We will never need to look around and search for God when troubles come. Even if we at first don't feel Him there, He is "present." We can take Him at His word—by faith, not feeling—and rest in His refuge and strength as storms rage around us. Verse seven confirms verse one with the words, *"The LORD of hosts is with us...."*

I also love verse ten which says, *"Be still, and know that I am God...."* In the raging storms of life, be still. In uncertainty, be still. When you do not feel the presence of God, be still—and know that He is God.

The Psalm ends with another affirmation of His continual presence: *"The LORD of hosts is with us..."* (v. 11a). Let's believe these promises and rest in the refuge and strength He provides.

# Psalm 47

VERSE ONE begins, *"Clap your hands, all ye people; shout unto God with the voice of triumph."* When I think of this verse, I think of cheering at sports events.

Do you like to watch sports? The sports of choice in the United States are generally football, basketball, or baseball. In Brazil, soccer is the sport of choice. What do we do when we watch? We clap and shout and cheer for our team.

The biggest soccer event every four years is the World Cup. Brazil is the only team in the world to have participated in every World Cup, and when the team plays, the stands are full of clapping and shouting people. I do not watch the Brazilian clubs play each other, but when the national team plays, I get excited. I promise myself I will sit quietly and watch, but that is a promise I do not keep. My family gets more entertainment out of watching my reactions than out of the game itself! But I am happy supporting my team.

God tells us in verse two why we should clap and shout. This Scripture says the following about the Lord: *"he is a great King over all the earth"* (v. 2b). The sports team we root for may be defeated, but our God is a great King Who is always "on top." We always have great reason to applaud Him and show our approval. Verse one commands us to shout with *"the voice of triumph,"* and our God is always triumphant.

We also need to use our voices to sing His praises. Four times in verse six, we are told to *"sing praises,"* and verse seven reinforces that command one more time. To me, praise seems to be quite important to God. I am not saying we need to sing a solo at church, but our voice should sing His praises when the congregation sings. How many times do we sound like we are singing a funeral dirge instead of praise to God in the church service?

Our God is great, and He is our King, so let's clap our hands, shout unto God with the voice of triumph, and sing praises to Him.

# Psalm 48

IN THIS Psalm, I want to focus on the first part of verse one: *"Great is the LORD and greatly to be praised."* This statement about our God is amazing.

The word *great,* which means "above average in ability or quality," is an apt description of our God. His omnipresence, omniscience, and omnipotence certainly place His abilities on a level higher than any human can even begin to imagine.

*Great* can also mean "important." God's importance is above everything and everyone. As Creator, He is above His creation in importance. As our Saviour, He should be more important than anything in our lives. Because He is great, we owe Him our praise.

The word *praise* has four meanings.

**Praise expresses approval.** We should show our approval to God for whatever He brings in our lives—even problems and difficulties. He tells us He works everything for our good if we love Him, so we should let Him know we accept what He brings into our lives. We tend to praise Him for what we like and what we think is good, but not for what we do not like.

**Praise also expresses admiration.** We often take God for granted and do not think much about Him during our day. But if we stop to look around us, we can see so much to admire—beautiful mountains, hills, rivers, animals. God created all of these with us in mind. Yes, I understand, if you live in a big city, you might need to take a drive or a vacation to see some of this beauty. He made the green grass, the beautiful flowers, the stately trees, and the blue sky with its ever-changing clouds. And He lovingly made us. Science learns more and more about the amazing intricacies of our bodies every day. We should show our admiration for God's marvelous works.

**Praise also expresses respect and gratitude.** For what greater gift do we have to be grateful than our salvation? When we come to Jesus asking forgiveness for our sins, He forgives us and gives us eternal life! Let's daily thank and praise Him for that indescribable gift!

**Praise can mean commendation.** We need to praise God to others, commending Him to them by sharing how they too can know this great God.

God is so great. Let's praise Him daily by showing our approval, admiration, and gratitude. Then lastly, let's commend this praiseworthy God to others.

# Psalm 49

WE ARE all tempted at times to look at successful and well-to-do people who are not interested in including God in their lives and be a little jealous of all they have. Certainly, being successful is not wrong, but making wealth, fame, and earthly possessions more important than serving God and following His principles is indeed wrong.

In the first three verses of this Psalm, the author is seeking everyone's attention. He says he will speak of wisdom and understanding. Then throughout the verses of this Psalm, he shows how every person will go to the grave and take nothing with him. Verse ten says both the wise man and the brutish man will die and leave all they have to others.

Of note is the psalmist's mention in verses six and seven that the wealthy cannot help redeem their brother. These verses remind me of the story Jesus told of the rich man and Lazarus, the poor, sick beggar who died and went to paradise. The rich man died and went to Hades. After unsuccessfully begging Abraham to send Lazarus to Him with a mere drop of water, he begged for someone to go and tell his brothers so they would not end up in that place of torment. But eternal choices must be made before the grave.

The psalmist mentions in verses 11 and 12 that men foolishly think their possessions will go on forever. Verse 13 says, *"This their way is their folly..."* and that *"the upright shall have dominion over them in the morning..."* (v. 14). The *upright* man is not one who is righteous in himself, but one who has asked the Lord to forgive him of his sins.

This Psalm teaches us not to be jealous of the ungodly with all of their possessions. The riches of the ungodly end at the grave, and then they will face eternity without God. But, as verse 15 says, *"God will redeem my soul from the power of the grave: for He shall receive me."* When we get to heaven, we will see that we chose the right path. Our riches are waiting there for us—if we have trusted God here.

Let's not focus on all that the unrighteous man has, for he will only leave it all behind. The good experiences of this man came to an end when ours are only beginning.

# $\mathfrak{P}$salm 50

I WANT TO focus on verses 14 and 15 in this Psalm. This passage can be divided into five different commands.

*"Offer unto God thanksgiving."* I love Thanksgiving! This holiday is a time to get together with family to enjoy a traditional turkey dinner with all the trimmings, as well as pumpkin pie. Hopefully, Thanksgiving should also be a time to give thanks and count our blessings. Originally, to give thanks was the purpose of the celebration—a time to be thankful for God's protection and provision. But so many times we forget to really be thankful or to express that thankfulness to God on this special day.

*"Pay thy vows unto the most High."* We usually do not focus our thoughts on God enough to even make any vows or promises to Him. But the psalmist reminds us that if we have done so, we need to keep our word. We don't like it when someone breaks a promise to us; therefore, we should be very careful not to do so with God. To promise Him something and not keep our word is a serious offense.

*"And call upon me in the day of trouble. "* We may not al-

ways be faithful, but God is. He does not promise to keep us from trouble, but He is always there to see us through the trouble. I especially like the poem "Footprints in the Sand," which tells of two sets of footprints side by side going along the beach. At one point, one set disappears during the most trying time in the person's life, and he asks God why he abandoned him.

The next phrase in this Psalm reflects the answer to the poet's question. *"I will deliver thee."* The answer was that God didn't abandon him. During that time of only one set of prints, God was carrying the person. He is always there for us.

The last phrase is, *"and thou shalt glorify me."* When troubles come in our life, they are not to make us miserable. Their purpose is two-fold: to draw us closer in dependence on God and to glorify Him. The very fact that God helped us will glorify Him, but God also wants us to testify of what He has done in our lives. So every Thanksgiving holiday, let's remember to thank God for His blessings, to keep our promises to Him, to call on Him in times of trouble, and when He answers, to glorify Him.

# $\mathfrak{P}$salm 51

Verse three says, *"Wash me throughly from mine iniquity, and cleanse me from my sin."* We each need to make this verse our prayer in order to have our sins forgiven and to receive the gift of salvation and a home in heaven. Once we seek His forgiveness, we cannot lose that salvation. The word *throughly* means we are thoroughly cleansed of every sin—past, present, and future. So why does the psalmist mention his sins over and over in this Psalm?

Verse ten says, *"Create in me a clean heart, O God."* Even after salvation, we do not become perfect. We should want to do right, but we still have the old nature that wants to do wrong. When we do wrong, we lose our fellowship with God, and asking forgiveness cleanses that spot on our heart and brings us close to God once more. When a child disobeys his parents, he does not stop being a son or a daughter, but the closeness of relationship is broken. When he says he is sorry, that closeness is restored. The same happens with us and our Heavenly Father.

Verse 12 says, *"Restore unto me the **joy** of thy salvation."* The psalmist did not lose His salvation when he sinned; rather, he lost the joy of being close to God. We should constantly examine our heart to see if there is a sin that is robbing our joy and then ask the Lord to remove the sin and restore the joy.

The psalmist experienced two results:

1) Verse 13 says, *"Then will I teach transgressors thy ways."* He wanted to tell others of this salvation and joy.

2) Verse 15 says, *"and my mouth shall shew forth thy praise."* The psalmist praised God after he got right with God.

Let's tell others about this wonderful forgiveness, and let's praise God for what He has done for us.

# Psalm 52

THE FIRST part of this Psalm describes the man who deals in mischief. The word *mischief,* which is used twice, can mean "harm, hurt, or injury." Some synonyms include "badness and misconduct," and this man is also described as "evil," and out of his mouth come lying, deceit, and devouring words. But before the psalmist finishes his description, he reminds this evil person that *"the goodness of God endureth continually"* (v. 1b). No matter how bad a person is, God's goodness is present, and He is ready to forgive that person if he repents.

But in verse five the psalmist also reminds the unrepentant man of a dreadful future: *"God shall likewise destroy thee for ever."* God will "root" him out of the land of the living because he *"made not God His strength"* (v. 7).

In contrast to uprooting the evil man, the psalmist compares himself to a green olive tree in the house of God, where it can receive God's blessings. The psalmist then lists three things he does, which we can also do, to grow as the green olive tree.

In verse eight, he expresses his trust in the mercy of God

---

forever. God's mercy alone saves us, and His mercy also restores us if we wander from Him.

Verse nine adds, *"I will praise thee for ever."* We should always be praising God for His salvation, mercy, and blessings.

Verse nine continues, *"I will wait on thy name; for it is good before thy saints."* God is always good, but sometimes we cannot see how He is working. Then is when we must wait and just trust in His goodness.

Let's be thankful for His mercy, praise Him, and wait on Him because He is always good.

# 𝔓salm 53

THIS PSALM is a sad description of the wickedness of men who are without God. Verse one describes them as being *corrupt* ("dishonest for monetary or personal gain") and indicts them for doing abominable iniquity—not simply sin, but evil and atrocity. Do these definitions sound like the world today?

God looked to find someone good and instead found people who were completely filthy. Twice the Psalm says that He found none that *"doeth good."* The Psalmist questions in verse four if they have any knowledge. But the problem is not that they are without knowledge, but that they *"have not called upon God"* (v. 4b).

Without God, none of us is good. We each have the choice to seek God or reject Him. To me, verse one is especially sad. *"The fool hath said in His heart, There is no God."* Rejecting God or denying the existence of God is incredibly foolish. If we acknowledge His existence, then it follows that we are accountable to Him and to His moral law. Men today do not want to face that reality, preferring to "do their own thing" and live for themselves.

Verse five reveals an interesting consequence of their decision: *"There were they in great fear, where no fear was...."* If we allow God in our lives and accept the Lord as our personal Saviour, our sin is forgiven, and we have fellowship with Him. We have no reason to fear eternity nor anything on this earth. But the ungodly have rejected God, and thus, they are subject to fears they would not need to have if they had God in their life.

Let's make sure we are part of the group who has called upon God, rather than the fool who decides there is no God or says no in defiance to God.

# $\mathfrak{P}$salm 54

T HIS PSALM begins with a plea: *"Save me, O God."* What we need saving from most is our sin. We are all sinners and cannot save ourselves, but God loves us and wants to forgive us if we come to Him in faith and then give us a future home in heaven.

But the psalmist mentions His enemies and says in verse three, *"they have not set God before them."* People who do not want God in their lives will always be at odds with Christians. The psalmist turns to God, and proclaims in verse four, *"Behold, God is mine helper."* God helped the psalmist and also wants to help us in whatever our difficulty.

Verse seven ends, *"For he hath delivered me out of all trouble...."* God also wants to be our helper and to free us from our troubles. Unfortunately, often we do not ask for His help. Have you ever watched a child continually ask His mother for something? Usually that child's continual nagging and begging yields the results he wants, but we often refrain from asking God for His help even one time. James 4:2 tells us we often do not have something because we simply do not ask.

In verse six the psalmist declares, *"I will praise thy name, O LORD; for it is good."* Let's ask God to save us—not just from our sins, but from our troubles. Let's trust Him to help us as He did the psalmist. Then let's remember to praise Him because He is good.

# 𝕻salm 55

DID YOU ever wish you could just run away and hide to escape from your problems or difficulties? After talking about his enemy, escape is exactly what the psalmist wishes he could do. He wants to fly away like a bird to escape from the storm and tempest in his life.

The worst part of his problem was not the enemy, but a dear friend who had turned against Him, making the adversity much harder to bear. But however difficult our problem is, the Lord wants to help us through it. In verses 16 and 17, the psalmist calls upon God, knowing and testifying that God will save him and hear him. In verse 18, resolution comes: *"He hath delivered my soul in peace from the battle that was against me."*

A contest was once announced to see who could paint the best picture depicting peace. Many pictures of beautiful, peaceful scenes were entered in the contest. But the winning picture was of a bird sitting on a nest in a tree with its wings spread over its babies, protecting them from a vicious buffeting rainstorm. God does not always protect us from the storms, but He shields us in them and gives us peace.

With this truth in mind, the psalmist declares, *"Cast thy burden upon the* LORD, *and he shall sustain thee: he shall never suffer the righteous to be moved"* (v. 22).

When we have a burden, we are so often like the hitchhiker who accepted a ride with a trucker. The man who needed a ride had been carrying a bag of potatoes that he continued to hold. The trucker said, "Hey, buddy, feel free to put your potatoes on the floor."

Instead of doing as the trucker bid, the hitchhiker replied, "Oh, no. It is enough that you are giving me a ride. I won't ask you to carry my potatoes too."

God wants us to give Him our burdens, but we often insist on carrying them ourselves. Let's let go of our burdens and allow the Lord to take them from us. If we do, we will be victorious over our problems, and God will help us to stand firm. We do not need to flee from our problems. God will graciously take them from us.

# $\mathfrak{P}$salm 56

$\mathbf{T}$HIS PSALM opens with the psalmist's asking God to be merciful. He felt like he was being swallowed up. Have you ever felt that way? Being swallowed up makes me think of the old Pacman arcade game, where the figure hurries through a maze gobbling up everything he finds in front of him while avoiding his enemies. Life can become complicated, and we might feel like we are being swallowed up in our problems. We need God's mercy to confront our enemies (problems) and gain victory over them as the psalmist did.

Confronting and resolving our problems can be frightening, but the psalmist says in verse three, *"What time I am afraid, I will trust in thee."* The moment we are overcome with fear because of the problems of life, we need to divert our attention from them to God. If we keep thinking of our problems and feel overwhelmed, our mind will not turn to God. We purposely need to turn our thoughts from the problem and replace that worry with thoughts of God. Trust that He is in control, that He loves us, and that He wants to help us.

In verse four, the psalmist again says he has put his trust

in God. But first He says, *"I will praise thy word."* Reading the Word of God will help us trust in God. We need to read it and meditate on what we have read, allowing it to penetrate our mind. As you read, ask yourself, "What principles do I see here to apply to my life? What promise is God giving me here? What is God showing me that I should take out of my life?" When we read His Word and apply it to our lives, our trust in Him will grow.

Again in verses ten and eleven, the psalmist says he will praise God's Word and trust in Him. This repetition shows how important God's Word is in our lives. The more we become "swallowed up" in His Word, the less we will feel "swallowed up" by the difficulties around us.

Let's praise His Word, and let's trust in the Lord.

# $\mathfrak{P}$salm 57

$I$N VERSE four, the psalmist cries, *"My soul is among lions: and I lie even among them that are set on fire."* This verse reminds me of two well-known Bible stories.

Daniel was a man of prayer who was known for praying three times a day to God. However, because he was a man in a high position, some subordinates were jealous. In order to undermine him, they tricked the king into instituting a law allowing people to pray only to the king. Those who did not follow the law were subject to a stiff penalty—death in the lions' den.

Daniel continued to pray to God in spite of the threat of the death penalty, and he was indeed thrown to the lions. The next morning the king was very happy to find Daniel unharmed because God had closed the mouths of the lions. His enemies were surprised by Daniel's survival, and as a result of their perfidy, suffered His intended fate in the lions' den.

The other story involved Daniel's three friends: Shadrach, Meshach, and Abednego. They were also faced with possible death if they remained faithful to God. A statue had been erected, and the king ordered everyone to bow down to it or be thrown into a fiery furnace. Regardless of the consequences, the three friends remained true to God and did not bow. After they were thrown in the furnace that had been heated seven times hotter than usual, the king saw another person with them that he said, *"the form of the fourth is like the Son of God"* (Daniel 3:25). The frightened king told them to come out, and the three men walked out of the furnace without even a trace of smoke. What an amazing act of deliverance for the three Hebrew friends to experience!

Daniel and his friends were faithful despite the possibility of death. How would we react in such a situation? Our faithfulness should be unconditional—not dependent on what the consequences could be. I am afraid many of us are unwilling to accept the consequences of being laughed at or put down because of our faith.

The psalmist declared, *"My heart is fixed, O God, my heart is fixed: I will sing and give praise"* (v. 7). Let's strive to keep our hearts and minds fixed on God and always ready to praise Him—even when all others seem to be against us.

# Psalm 58

EVERY YEAR and even every day as I look at events in the world, the world seems to move farther and farther from God and the principles in His Word. The wicked seem to be taking over in politics, business, and every area of life. With so much that seems to be wrong in the world, I feel sometimes like the psalmist as he addresses the wicked.

In verse two he describes them as follows: *"Yea, in heart ye work wickedness...."* In verse three, he says they go astray as soon as they are born! In verse four, he asserts they are as poison. Then he talks about how he would like to see them destroyed. I know we are supposed to "hate the sin but love the sinner," and on a personal level, I would love to see everyone turn to God. But if they don't, then I do not want their poison to continue to spread! God also wants everyone to come to Him, but if they do not turn from their wickedness, they will be judged.

Verses ten and eleven bring matters to a conclusion as the psalmist says that righteousness will be restored. *"The righteous shall rejoice when he seeth the vengeance...So that a man shall say, Verily there is a reward for the righteous: verily he is a God that judgeth in the earth."*

So don't be disheartened when you see the evil in the world. God will judge though His judgment may not be in our timing. It may not even be in this lifetime, but God will at some point make everything right. The ungodly will be judged, and we will one day receive rewards for our righteous living.

Let's always remember that God will judge the wicked and He will reward the righteous. Let's keep our eyes on the Lord and let Him take care of the wicked.

# Psalm 59

ERSE 16 of this Psalm says, *"But I will sing of thy power; yea, I will sing aloud of thy mercy in the morning: for thou hast been my defense and refuge in the day of my trouble."* In this Psalm, I see four key words to consider.

## Power

One definition of *power* is "the capacity to direct or influence the behavior of others or the course of events." Being omnipotent, or all-powerful, God certainly is able to do as He wishes in the lives of people or in the process of events. The psalmist had been addressing his enemies and knew that God could deal with them in the way He chose. The Bible also tells us that God controls even the heart of kings, so the psalmist had no reason to fear his enemies. We can have this same confidence in the power of God in our lives.

## Mercy

*Mercy* is defined as "compassion or forgiveness shown toward someone whom it is within one's power to harm." God is merciful to anyone who comes to Him for forgiveness of their sins. But once God forgives us and gives us salvation, we disappoint Him so many times. Even then He is always ready to show mercy and work in our lives. The psalmist said he would sing of God's mercy in the morning. Every morning when we rise, we should think of the many ways God shows His mercy to us and praise Him. God showed His mercy by being the psalmist's defense and refuge.

## Defense

*Defense* is "protection or support against attack." If we will ask, God will protect us from the attacks of the Devil. In and of ourselves we are weak, but God is a support and will hold us up against the Enemy's attack. Some people critically call Christianity a crutch. Well, Christ is much more than a mere crutch, but I see nothing bad about using a crutch when one is needed. I broke my leg in high school playing soccer in gym class. For six weeks I was very glad to have crutches to help me get around! I could have done nothing without them. The Lord is our *crutch*, or "support," when we cannot stand on our own.

## Refuge

A *refuge* is "a condition of being safe or sheltered from pursuit, danger, or trouble." How wonderful to feel safe and sheltered from the storms of life! Let's rest in the Lord and feel His protective arms around us.

# Psalm 60

*I* WANT TO focus primarily on four phrases in two verses of this Psalm.

*"Give us help from trouble"* (v. 11). We all face trouble in our life—sometimes because of our foolish choices and sometimes because trouble is a part of life. God never promises the Christian a "bed of roses." Sometimes life simply is not easy. But the psalmist knew what to do when trouble came: he asked God for help. So many times we do everything we can think of to help resolve a situation. When nothing works, only then do we think to ask God for help. We need to learn to come to God first for His wisdom.

*"For vain is the help of man"* (v. 11). We should not depend on ourselves nor others to solve our problems. That does not mean God cannot use others to help us; we should not look to men and think that all we need is their knowledge and help to meet all our needs.

*"Through God we shall do valiantly"* (v. 12). I love this precious promise. *Valiant* means "courageous or brave." We are not courageous or brave because of ourselves. We are valiant

through God alone. So before we trust in ourselves or others, we need to place our trust in God—the only One worthy of our complete trust. When we look to Him, He can give us wisdom or give others wisdom to help us, but our help is all "through God." Why do we need to go through Him? The fourth and final phrase of this passage tells us why.

*"For He it is that shall tread down our enemies"* (v. 12). The psalmist knew where his help would come from. That's why he appealed in verse 5, *"save with thy right hand, and hear me."* I am sure God could use either hand to deliver us, but most people are right-handed, so their right hand is stronger. I think the verse is showing that God will save with all His strength. That same God will hear us and deliver us—whatever our problem. Let's not look to ourselves or depend on the help of man. Let's turn to God for our help when we have a need or problems come.

# $\mathfrak{P}$salm 61

I N VERSE one, the psalmist is crying to the Lord in prayer, but verse two contains some interesting added statements.

*"From the end of the earth will I cry unto thee...."* No matter where we are, we can call upon the Lord. When we left the States to come to Brazil as missionaries, God did not stop hearing me. Cell phones can be a blessing, but they can be very aggravating when you are in a place with no reception. But God's lines are open to hear us from anywhere when we call on Him.

The psalmist adds in verse two, *"when my heart is overwhelmed...."* Have you ever felt like you were so overcome by a situation that you did not even know how to pray? You could not find the words to put your emotions or thoughts in a cohesive request to offer to God. Not having the right words or even any words at all doesn't matter. We can come to God and tell Him we do not know what to say or how to pray but ask Him to read our heart. The Bible says the Holy Spirit takes our prayers to God and "interprets" them for us. God knows us better than we know ourselves, and He knows our hearts when we are too overwhelmed to express ourselves correctly or coherently.

The psalmist concludes the verse by imploring, *"lead me to the rock that is higher than I."* When we feel overwhelmed, we can trust God to lift us above the problem and set us on a rock. We need to let God lead us, rather than depend on our own wisdom to solve matters.

Verse three states, *"For thou hast been a shelter for me...."* Whether or not we are overwhelmed, God is always there to shelter us from the storms and trials of life and even from the day-by-day seemingly petty problems we all encounter.

In verse four the psalmist includes two more helpful thoughts. He said he would abide in God's tabernacle. We also get strength by abiding in God's house. At church we have the fellowship and encouragement of others to help us, as well as the preaching of God's Word to strengthen us. The psalmist also trusted in the covert of God's wings. The covert feathers on a bird cover other feathers. One set of covert feathers protects the ears. Essentially the covert feathers cover and protect the wing and tail feathers. God protects us as a hen covers her chicks with her wings and tail feathers or coverts.

Wherever we are, let's remember God is there. Let's seek and take shelter in Him.

# $\mathfrak{P}$salm 62

$\mathcal{V}$ERSE FIVE of this Psalm says, "*My soul, wait thou only upon God; for my expectation is from him.*" Have you ever expected something and then been disappointed? Maybe you expected a certain Christmas or birthday gift but did not receive it. Or you expected something to happen, even antici-pated it, but the event did not take place.

When we were on deputation getting ready to go to Bra-zil, we visited one of my husband's brothers for Christmas and fully expected our visas to be awaiting us when we returned home. We arrived home only to find that the officials wanted more paperwork! We did not finally get our visas until May. People or situations often disappoint us because our expecta-tions are not fulfilled.

The psalmist said he waited only on God and then instructs us to do likewise: wait only on God. He states that God is his salvation, rock, defense, and refuge. We can also expect God to be the same for us.

The psalmist also says he will not be moved. We have the same firm foundation as the psalmist did, and we can expect

God to hold us. Having our expectation in God does not mean we can expect Him to give us everything we might wish for. We can surely trust God to be everything He says He is.

Man will disappoint us and fail us, but God never fails. Verse 11 says, *"God hath spoken once; twice have I heard this; that power belongeth unto God."* The psalmist emphasizes doubly that God is powerful. Let's do as verse eight says, *"Trust in him at all times; ye people, pour out your heart before him: God is a refuge for us."* Let's put our expectation in Him.

# ℙsalm 63

In verse one, the psalmist addresses seeking God early. By seeking Him early, we have His presence with us all day long. I know finding much extra time in the morning can be hard, especially for mothers with small children. When my children were small, seemingly no matter what time I tried to get up, one of the kids would wake up too! But taking even a minute to at least read one verse and take that verse with you in your mind throughout the day can be a great blessing.

The psalmist talked about seeking God as one who was thirsty where no water was! In my mind's eye, I can picture someone staggering and crawling across the desert toward an oasis, seeking water. Are we as eager to seek God as that person seeking water at that oasis?

The psalmist then talks about God's power and glory. Perhaps focusing on the wonderful attributes of our God will develop a thirst within us to spend more time with Him. The psalmist said God's lovingkindness was better than life! *Lovingkindness* is "kindness or affectionate behavior resulting from or expressing love." God shows His kindness and love toward us in many ways. Because of this, the psalmist said he would bless God and his mouth would praise Him with joyful lips. Then he adds in verse six, *"When I remember thee upon my bed, and meditate on thee in the night watches."*

So the psalmist started his day seeking God early, praised him throughout the day as he thought on God's goodness in his life, and meditated more on the Lord at night as he lay down to rest. Let's do the same as the psalmist, keeping the Lord in focus throughout the day from morning to night.

# Psalm 64

THE PSALMIST begins this Psalm by calling upon God because of his enemies. In seeking God, he makes an interesting comment: *"Preserve my life from fear of the enemy"* (v. 1b). Not only can God give us victory over our enemies, but He can also give us victory over our fear of them. At times we might pray for God to give us victory over our problems and difficulties, but until we see the victory, we may still have fear in our heart. But if we know that God gives the victory, we do not have to hold on to the fear in our hearts though the results remain uncertain.

The psalmist continues in the Psalm to address his enemies as being without fear and shooting their arrows. Then verse seven paints an interesting picture: *"But God shall shoot at them with an arrow; suddenly shall they be wounded."* The enemy may sometimes seem to have the upper hand, but God is the ultimate victor. Of course, God did not shoot literal arrows, and neither are our battles fought with literal bows and arrows. But just as God defeated the psalmist's enemies, He is with us to defeat our Enemy, the Devil, and the problems that come into our lives.

This passage shares two results from this victory. First, in verse nine, the psalmist said, *"And all men shall fear, and shall declare the work of God."* When God takes away our fear, our enemies will fear and will know that the victory we have found is the work of God.

The second result is found in verse ten which says, *"The righteous shall be glad in the LORD, and shall trust him; and all the upright in heart shall glory."* As other Christians see how God gives us victory, they will be glad for us, also give God the glory, and trust Him to help them too.

Let's turn our fear over to God, knowing He will give us victory. Let's be glad in the Lord and trust Him. Thus, we will receive victory, and others can rejoice with us in the victory God has given.

# Psalm 65

VERSE five begins, *"By terrible things in righteousness wilt thou answer us...."* We usually think of the word *terrible* as meaning something horrible. But in relation to God, I think of the word as meaning "causing awe." The previous verses referred to man's iniquity and transgressions but state God will purge them away. When God fulfills this promise, we will receive His righteousness. We certainly should be awed that God in His love would do that for us. Our salvation is an amazing gift that should make us stand in awe before God!

The verse continues with *"O God of our salvation; who art the confidence of all the ends of the earth, and of them that are afar off upon the sea."* Whether we are at one end of the earth or completely around the globe at the other end or somewhere in the middle of the ocean, we can have confidence in God. He reaches us wherever we are in the world and in whatever position we are facing in our life.

*Confidence* means "full trust; belief in the power, trustworthiness, or reliability of a person or thing." We can fully trust in God and rest in all three of these characteristics of

confidence—power, trustworthiness, and reliability—in relation to God.

**First, God is all-powerful.** The next verses show His power
in nature. God has power over everyone and anything, so we
can count on Him to give us strength and power to overcome
our problems.

**Second, God is trustworthy.** Friends and acquaintances
can let us down and disappoint us, but God is worthy of our
trust. As we trust Him for salvation, we can trust Him to lead
and guide us each day.

**Finally, God is reliable.** I love the chorus,

> *"Jesus never fails; Jesus never fails.*
> *Heaven and earth may pass away,*
> *But Jesus never fails."*

We may experience earthquakes and tsunamis, and sometimes
"falling stars," but Jesus will never fail. He is always there for us.

Let's put our confidence totally in Him, always remembering His power, trustworthiness, and reliability.

# ℘salm 66

Praise is a recurring theme throughout the Psalms. This Psalm starts by telling us, *"Make a joyful noise unto God, all ye lands: Sing forth the honour of his name: make his praise glorious"* (vv. 1, 2).

The psalmist says to make a *joyful* noise—not necessarily a *beautiful* sound. I don't sing in the shower, but I love to listen to beautiful Christian music, and sometimes I sing along. As we listen to the words and think about them, the music can lift our hearts to praise the Lord. Music helps us think about God's greatness and all His blessings on us.

The last three verses of the Psalm turn our thoughts to another theme. Verses 18 through 20 say, *"If I regard iniquity in my heart, the Lord will not hear me: But verily God hath heard me; he hath attended to the voice of my prayer. Blessed be God, which hath not turned away my prayer, nor his mercy from me."*

I want to address three thoughts from this passage.

**First, if we have unconfessed sin in our heart, God will not hear our prayers.** If we are holding sin in our heart and refuse to let go of it, God will not listen and answer our prayers.

141

**Secondly, if we confess the sin that is in our heart, then God promises to hear us, and He will answer our prayers.** God does have three answers: yes, no, and wait. He will answer with what is best for us. He knows that it is sometimes best to say no or that the time is not right, waiting to give us our request in a little while.

**Thirdly, whatever God answers, we need to bless Him for it.** Sometimes we ask for things, and we forget to thank Him when He answers our prayers. We need to thank Him and bless Him for answering and for showing His mercy to us.

Let's examine our lives and confess any sin in our hearts and then come to God with our requests. Then let's praise and bless the Lord for His answers to prayer and for His mercy in our lives.

# $\mathfrak{P}$salm 67

THE WORD *praise,* which is used several times in this Psalm, means "**admiration** or **approval**; to express one's **respect** and **gratitude**." Let's examine four words in this definition.

## Admiration —
### "pleasurable contemplation"

Contemplating on, or deeply thinking about, the attributes of our great God will certainly lead us to praise Him. He is loving, kind, forgiving, all-powerful, and all-knowing to name only a few. Going beyond His being to also look at His creation will certainly be pleasurable. Looking at the beauty in the mountains, hills, skies, and lakes is amazing. When considering the intricacies of the animal world and our human bodies, we cannot help but admire God for what He is and for His creation.

## Approval—
### "the belief that something is good or acceptable"

This Psalm says twice that God will bless us, and He often blesses us with health and prosperity, which we consider good. At other times, we might have health problems or feel less than

144 | GERRI JOHNSON

prosperous, but He has said in His Word that all things work together for our good. We might not like all He brings into our life, but if we believe His Word, we can accept anything because God says it is good. Thus we can approve of what He knows is for our good.

## Respect—
### *"deference"*

We may not understand everything God allows in our life, but if we respect Him as the all-knowing God, we will realize that everything is for our good and has a reason. So, we defer to God's choices and accept His will in our life.

## Gratitude—
### *"feeling appreciation"*

If we truly defer to His will and want His choices for our life, we will be grateful for whatever—the good and the bad—God brings into our lives. Let's gratefully accept everything that happens as being from God's hand.

Let's praise God daily by showing Him our admiration, approval, respect, and gratitude.

# Psalm 68

**V**ERSE three says, *"But let the righteous be glad; let them rejoice before God: yea, let them exceedingly rejoice."* I don't know if you like sports, but the words *"exceedingly rejoice"* make me think of people cheering at a game. When my husband was in seminary, we would go to the school team's basketball games when we could, and we especially liked the games with our "archenemy." The games were always close, often decided by a point or two in the last few minutes. The cheering went on throughout the entire game!

How often do we show anywhere near that kind of emotion when we think of our God and the marvels He has done? Verse four repeats the challenge to *extol* (praise exceedingly) God. The next verses include many examples of what God has done, giving us great reason to praise Him. He helps the fatherless, the widows, the solitary, and the poor.

The psalmist mentions the many ways God helped the Israelites as they journeyed to the Promised Land and then after they had settled in the land. God also gives us many victories as we journey through life. Let's praise Him for those victories.

If we had no other reason to praise God, verse 20 gives us an unforgettable one: *"He that is our God is the God of salvation...."* Some people try to say that the paths to heaven are many, but the Bible teaches that God is the only way, through faith in His Son Jesus Christ and His dying on the cross for our sins. *"Jesus saith unto Him, I am the way, the truth, and the life: no man cometh unto the Father, but by me"* (John 14:6). If we have accepted His gift of salvation, then we have the promise of a home in heaven forever. If salvation were the only blessing we ever received, it would be enough for us to want to *exceedingly* praise God!

Let's *"exceedingly rejoice"* in what God has done for us and say with the psalmist in verse 35, *"Blessed be God."*

# 𝔓salm 69

𝖁ERSE 13a SAYS, *"But as for me, my prayer is unto thee, O Lord, in an acceptable time."* When is an acceptable time? Anytime is acceptable because the book of Philippians tells us to *"Pray without ceasing."* God's ear is always ready to hear us pray. But let's look at some of the times the psalmist mentions.

Verse 5, *"O God, thou knowest my foolishness; and my sins are not hid from thee."* We all are foolish at times (or, at least, I am)—either committing a sin we shouldn't have or doing something stupid that brings problems into our lives. An acceptable time to pray for God's forgiveness and help is when we have sinned or done something foolish.

Verse 19, *"Thou hast known my reproach, and my shame, and my dishonour...."* Anytime we have done something to cause shame or dishonor is an acceptable time to pray. God wants to restore us.

Verse 20, *"Reproach hath broken my heart...."* Whatever the cause, anytime we have a broken heart is an acceptable time to pray. God loves us and wants to bind up our broken heart.

Verse 29, *"But I am poor and sorrowful...."* Whether we are poor in spirit and need a lift or are facing a financial or physical need, these are acceptable times to pray. Another acceptable time to pray is when we are sad because of a loss or a difficult time in our life.

Let's pray, and when God answers, let's say with the psalmist in verse 30: *"I will praise the name of God with a song, and will magnify him with thanksgiving."*

# Psalm 70

THE FIRST three verses of this Psalm are asking for deliverance from those wanting the psalmist hurt. I want to focus on the last two verses of this short Psalm.

Verse four begins, *"Let all those that seek thee rejoice and be glad in thee...."* The first thing a person needs to seek God for is salvation. Without His salvation, all else is vain, and He is the right One to go to when seeking salvation. After finding salvation in Him, we can still seek Him for help in time of trouble or for guidance in our daily life. Whatever the reason we are seeking Him, we need to rejoice and be glad when He has answered. So often we ask for things and forget to thank Him when He answers.

The verse continues, *"and let such as love thy salvation say continually, Let God be magnified."* We should never "get over" the wonderful gift of salvation. We should continually remember what He did for us when He saved us and magnify Him because of it.

In verse five the psalmist says, *"But I am poor and needy: Make haste unto me, O God. Thou art my help and deliverer; O*

LORD, *make no tarrying.*" We all feel needy at times. The psalmist knew where to turn in his need. He declared that the Lord was his help. When we try to do things on our own, we often fail. Sometimes we do not like to ask for help—either from others or from God. But we need to humble ourselves and seek help when we need it.

The psalmist also said God was his deliverer. Sometimes we will ask someone for help, and the person might even try to help, but he will not be successful. But if we ask God, we can know He is able to help.

Let's be like the psalmist and ask for help when we need it. Let's trust God to be our help and deliverer.

# ℘salm 71

SOMETIMES WE see someone who loved and served God in his or her younger years but then fell away or lost that interest when older. As I grow older, I look around and see that happening to acquaintances and people I grew up with and have known through the years.

Verse one of this Psalm begins, *"In thee, O LORD, do I put my trust: let me never be put to confusion."* The psalmist is saying that the Lord has been his hope and trust since his youth, and he asks that his mouth be filled with his praise and honor all the day.

Then in verse nine he requests, *"Cast me not off in the time of old age; forsake me not when my strength faileth."* When his physical strength began to fail because of age, he did not want to be set aside but desired to continue to serve and praise God. Paul, in the New Testament, expressed this same fear in saying he did not want to be a castaway.

But the psalmist knew that a lack of physical strength as a person ages is not what generally keeps him from serving God. He prayed in verse 12, *"O God, be not far from me: O my God, make haste for my help."* Rather, keeping our eyes on the Lord allows us to be faithful into our older years.

The psalmist said He would praise God more and more. Verse 15 says, *"My mouth shall shew forth thy righteousness and thy salvation all the day; for I know not the numbers thereof."* None of us know how long we will live, so we need to take advantage of every day to serve and praise God. And if He gives us many years, we need to resolve to remain faithful.

In verse nine, the psalmist talks about his strength failing, but a few verses later in verse sixteen, he remembers where to get strength: *"I will go in the strength of the Lord God...."*

In verse 17 the psalmist remembers how God taught him in his youth, and in verse 18, he again asks God not to forsake him in his old age.

Let's be like the psalmist, taking advantage of each day to serve God throughout our life and asking God to keep us faithful into our older years. We will also be able to say, *"My tongue also shall talk of thy righteousness all the day long..."* (v. 24a). Let's speak of Him every day until the end of our days. Let's depend on the Lord's strength to keep us faithful.

# Psalm 72

Many different kings and heads of government have ruled the nations of the world through the centuries. Some have been good leaders, and some have been anything but good. Some have brought peace for a time, and others have brought war and turmoil. But eventually, their rule is passed on to another. A great deal of this Psalm addresses the time when Jesus will return to rule on the earth. What a wonderful reign it will be! Those of us who are Christians will be part of this time of peace and plenty.

He will care for the poor and needy (v. 4).

The righteous will flourish, and there will be peace (v. 7). How good to know that right and peace will rule rather than injustice and turmoil!

Every king will serve Him (v. 11). The whole world will be ruled in justice.

He will deliver from deceit and violence and bring plentiful harvests (vv. 12-16). What a different and wonderful world that will be!

*"His name shall endure for ever: His name shall be continued as*

*long as the sun: and men shall be blessed in him: all nations shall call him blessed"* (v. 17). The next two verses also talk about blessing God and His wonderful name. But we do not need to wait until God rules in His kingdom to bless and praise Him. We certainly do not live in a perfect world, but if we have Him reigning in our hearts, we have peace and joy in our lives— even though the world may be filled with violence and turmoil. We also have the hope of that glorious kingdom in the future.

So, like the psalmist, let's rejoice and say, *"Blessed be his glorious name for ever"* (v. 19a).

# $\mathfrak{P}$salm 73

$\mathfrak{H}$OW MANY times are we tempted to look at those who seem to have everything—a beautiful house, a new car, a lucrative job—and be envious? We wonder why the wicked and unjust have everything and we have nothing in comparison. According to verse three, the psalmist was envious of the foolish. But the words used to describe the foolish are not very complimentary—*foolish, wicked, prideful, corrupt.* They had, as verse seven said, *"more than heart could wish,"* but their hearts were turned against God.

As he took note of them, the psalmist first wondered why he was even concerned about keeping his heart clean, but then he finally saw the truth. He said, *"Until I went into the sanctuary of God; then understood I their end. Surely thou didst set them in slippery places: thou castedst them down into destruction"* (vv. 17, 18). Whatever the ungodly have now will all be lost.

This Psalm sheds much light on the story Jesus told of the rich man and the poor Lazarus. Lazarus had nothing—not even his health. The rich man had everything. When both died, the rich man suffered in hell with not even water to quench his thirst, while Lazarus enjoyed Paradise.

When we focus on what the wicked have in this life, we can become jealous and unhappy. When we focus on God and walk close to Him, we have joy in His presence and the hope of eternity in heaven, where our riches are being stored for us if we are serving Him while here. In verse 22 the psalmist called himself *foolish*, which is what we also are if we focus on the riches of the ungodly.

The psalmist turned his focus back to God and said in verse 25, *"Whom have I in heaven but thee? And there is none upon earth that I desire beside thee."*

Let's change our focus from the world to God. Let's say like the psalmist, *"But it is good for me to draw near to God: I have put my trust in the Lord GOD, that I may declare all thy works"* (v. 28).

# ℘salm 74

THE PSALMIST begins by asking God to remember His people and then describing all of the destruction Israel had
suffered at the hand of their enemies. In verse nine he says,
*"We see not our signs: there is no more any prophet."* The people
could not see the signs from God of His displeasure with them,
and the prophets were no longer advising the people to repent
so God could bless them again.

To me this Psalm pictures America today. We are quickly
leaving our Christian foundations, and our nation is being destroyed from within. We don't see the signs of God's displeasure or His withholding of blessings from us. We might ask as
the psalmist, *"O God, how long shall the adversary reproach?
shall the enemy blaspheme thy name for ever?"* (v. 10).

But the psalmist still remembered the greatness of God
when he said, *"For God is my King of old, working salvation in
the midst of the earth"* (v. 12). God is still working in individual
lives. He will give salvation to anyone who turns to Him. But
we need to pray for the salvation of our nation. Pray that this
country will turn back to its Christian foundation.

In verses 16 and 17, we are reminded that God is the Creator of everything—day and night, summer and winter. He has power to do anything, but because He gives us free will, He allows us to choose our path. We need to pray that the people of our land will choose to walk in God's path. Then He can and will bless us as a nation again.

Let's remember our nation, praying for her throughout the day, every day. Let's pray for the nation as a whole to turn back to God and pray that individuals will give their lives to the Lord. Let's covenant to pray with our family that God will bless our land and its people.

# Psalm 75

VERSE ONE says, *"Unto thee, O God, do we give thanks, unto thee do we give thanks: for that thy name is near thy wondrous works declare."* Have you ever done something for someone, and the person did not thank you? Maybe you gave someone a gift and never received a thank-you note. We generally don't like it when we are not thanked or appreciated for something we have done.

God has given us this wonderful world with all the beauty of nature. Maybe when He created strawberries, He thought, *I think My people will enjoy these.* He made everything for man to manage and enjoy. All of God's amazing works have His name written in them. When we see creation, we can see God. But do we often think to thank Him for His great work? When we see a beautiful waterfall, do we say, "That is beautiful! Thank You, God, for making this waterfall for us to enjoy"?

Unfortunately, because of man and his sin, we live in an imperfect world. So the tone of the Psalm changes and verses six and seven say, *"For promotion cometh neither from the east, nor from the west, nor from the south. But God is the judge: he putteth down one, and setteth up another.*" So whatever comes our way in this beautiful but imperfect world, remember that God is in control. If you think matters are unfair, leave them in God's hands. He controls everything, and He can put anyone "in his place" if He needs to.

So this Psalm teaches us a couple of principles:

1) Let's be thankful for the wonderful world God gave us.

2) Let's leave things in God's hands when we don't feel they are fair. Let Him be the judge. Whatever comes our way, let's say as the psalmist in verse nine: *"But I will declare for ever; I will sing praises to the God of Jacob."*

# Psalm 76

THIS PSALM starts, *"In Judah is God known: his name is great in Israel."* His name was known because the people had seen all of the wonders God did as He brought them out of Egypt and delivered them to the Promised Land. The psalmist mentions how God broke the defense of the enemy. Verse six mentions how the chariots and horses were destroyed. God did that for Israel when the Egyptian army came in pursuit. God opened the Red Sea, let His people cross on dry ground, and then covered the Egyptian horses and chariots that followed with the waters of the sea He had parted, drowning the entire army.

What a wonderful story most of us heard as children! But do we think about that event as actually happening? The crossing of the Red Sea is not a fairy tale, but a miraculous event. God gave victory to His people, and He still gives us victory today when we trust Him. If Israel had simply stood still with the Red Sea before them, the enemy would have overtaken them. But they went forward by faith, and God gave them deliverance. God is also ready to help us today. We may seem overwhelmed by the problems of life that the Devil sends our way. But verse seven says, *"Thou, even thou, art to be feared: and who may stand in thy sight when once thou art angry?"* The Devil cannot stand or prevail in God's presence. If we will allow God to fight for us, we can have the same victory Israel had.

But there is a price. Verse 11 says, *"Vow, and pay unto the LORD your God: let all that be round about him bring presents unto him that ought to be feared."* What present does He want from us? He wants every believer's life as a living sacrifice. Just as Israel followed God out of Egypt, we need to follow God with our life. Let's determine to follow Him in whatever His will is for our life, and let's watch Him defeat our enemies as we follow Him.

# Psalm 77

Have you ever felt like your whole world was caving in? The psalmist seems to be describing this type of circumstance in the beginning of this Psalm. Verse three lists three ways the psalmist was headed down a path to disaster.

**First, the psalmist was troubled.** He allowed himself to be concerned about the situation surrounding him instead of resting in God and turning the situation over to Him. In verse six he says he was communing with his own heart and his spirit made diligent search. He was trying to analyze the matter himself, when all He needed to do was give the problem to God.

**Second, the psalmist complained.** I can imagine his thinking about his world caving in around him as he examined the circumstances in his heart. I can hear him saying, *"God, where are You? What are You doing in my life?"* I can imagine that because I am also tempted to complain when things go wrong. Complaining is so easy.

**Third, the psalmist's spirit was overwhelmed.** Complaining and seeing the negative in every situation usually lead to feeling overwhelmed. If we will say, "God, I don't understand, but I trust You. Work Your will in this situation and bring glory to Yourself," we can come through the difficulty, trusting God and feeling calm. If we do not trust Him, then we are stressed and overwhelmed, not knowing where to turn.

But then the psalmist came to His senses and declared, *"I will remember the works of the LORD: surely I will remember thy wonders of old"* (v. 11). The psalmist decided to stop and think about all of the wonderful things God had done in the past.

God still does wonderful things in our lives. When difficulties come and despair threatens to rear its ugly head, like the psalmist, we need to remember all of the great things God has done for us in the past.

In verse 12 the psalmist said, *"I will meditate also of all thy work, and talk of thy doings."* He thought of what God had done in the past, meditated on it, and talked about it. Let's follow the same formula to defeat despair.

# Psalm 78

THE PSALMIST asks us to listen to Him in this Psalm as He tells of all that God did for Israel. The future generations would need to remember and continue to praise God for what He had done. He retells all that God did in Egypt to force Pharaoh to allow the people of Israel to leave, as well as all He did as they travelled in the wilderness—providing water, food, and protection. Yet the people continually forgot how God had blessed them and turned to complaining, unbelief, and other gods.

Finally, in disgust, God would "slay" them. He would turn them over to their enemies. In their trouble, they would turn back to God. I am always amazed at how the people of Israel would keep turning away and forgetting how God had helped them in the past. But then I think how we often do the same. Over and over, we doubt God—just like the Israelites did.

Verse 35 says, *"And they remembered that God was their rock, and the high God their redeemer."* When God gets our attention, we remember Him again. But the next verses say, *"Nevertheless they did flatter him with their mouth, and they lied unto him with their tongues. For their heart was not right with him, neither were they steadfast in his covenant."* Are we like the Israelites and only give God "lip service"? We might go to church and even talk about God, but we are not really following Him with our whole heart.

Yet the next verses tell how God forgives His people repeatedly and does not judge them. Verse 38 says God was full of compassion and forgave their iniquity. But the Psalm continues by telling how they turned from God repeatedly until He finally turned them over to their enemies.

God is a loving and forgiving God, but a point comes when He will judge. Let's learn our lesson from the nation of Israel and decide we will trust God and follow Him with our whole heart. Let's not just give Him lip service but follow Him completely with our whole heart.

# Psalm 79

VERSE EIGHT says, *"O remember not against us former iniquities: let thy tender mercies speedily prevent us: for we are brought very low."* When we come to the Lord and ask Him to forgive our sins and save us, we receive a home in heaven and the gift of eternal life that we cannot lose. But we do not become perfect, and though we should want to do right, we will sin and do wrong at times. We are still saved and on our way to heaven, but as a result of our sin, our fellowship with God is broken.

When we sin, we can sometimes keep remembering the things we have done wrong—even if we have asked for forgiveness. Such is the situation of the psalmist in this chapter. He asks God not to remember the things he has done because he constantly remembers them. Reliving these memories is disheartening, bringing him low (v. 8). He asks God in His mercy to keep him from remembering.

Once we ask for forgiveness, we should always remember that our sin is forgotten in the eyes of God. We should not keep beating ourselves up over past sin that has already been forgiven. We need to accept God's forgiveness and move on in life.

The psalmist says, *"So we thy people and sheep of thy pasture will give thee thanks for ever: we will shew forth thy praise to all generations"* (v. 13). I love the analogy of God's people and sheep—helpless creatures, often disobeying the shepherd and getting lost or in trouble. We do the same—sinning against God or causing difficulties in our life. But we simply need to do as the psalmist and ask God to help in His mercy. When we do, He helps us! We need to remember to thank and praise Him for His intervention and help.

Let's be like the psalmist and show forth His praise to all generations.

# 𝔓salm 80

THIS PSALM begins by addressing the Lord as a shepherd. A shepherd has always had many jobs, one of which was guiding the sheep to new pastures. Verse one says, *"thou that leadest Joseph like a flock."* Sheep are not self-sufficient animals and need a shepherd to guide them and provide watchcare for them. Like sheep, we can also get lost and become confused in life if we try to go our own way. The principles of the Bible are to be our guide through life, but we often turn away to what seems to be greener pastures. Israel did, and most of this Psalm describes their troubles because of turning from God's ways.

Three times (vv. 3, 7, 19) the psalmist says, *"Turn us again."* Many times we need to turn from going our own way to once again follow God. Then we will be saved from the mess we make of our lives when we choose our own path.

A shepherd is also a watchman. He is vigilant to watch for animals of prey that might want to harm the sheep. The Bible says of Satan that he is a roaring lion, seeking whom he may devour. As the shepherd wants to protect his helpless sheep, the Lord wants to protect us from Satan.

Another job of the shepherd is that of savior. Sheep are unable to defend themselves against attack, so the shepherd is prepared to kill any animal that attacks them. The Lord delivers us from Satan when we come to Him, trusting only in Him for our salvation. But He continues to save us from the snares of Satan throughout our life by pointing out the Devil's traps through His Word and giving us the Holy Spirit to strengthen us as we defeat the purposes of Satan.

A shepherd is also a provider as he leads the sheep to the best pastures and to calm waters. But the sheep have to follow him. If they seek greener grass, they will get lost. The Lord also promises to provide for His people. He meets our physical needs.

Let's turn to the Lord and trust Him to meet our every need.

# ℙsalm 81

SOMETIMES WE wonder why our lives are in such chaos or why this world has so many problems and difficulties. Some people try to blame God for their problems when in reality, the problem is with us.

In this Psalm, God tells how He answered Israel when the people called upon Him. Verse seven says, *"Thou callest in trouble, and I delivered thee."* But several verses later in verse 11, God declares, *"But my people would not hearken to my voice."* Once again, Israel soon forgot God.

We believers often act in exactly the same way. The problem is that many times when we don't know where else to turn, we call on God. He helps us, but after a while when things are going well, we tend to forget Him.

God instructed Israel to have no other gods before them, but they did not listen. Verse 11 says, *"But my people would not hearken to my voice...."* Their problems were not God's fault, but their own for turning from God's help. Verse 12 says, *"So I gave them up unto their own hearts' lust: and they walked in their own counsel."* When they refused to listen to God, He let them follow their own desires. Like the children of Israel, He will also allow us to do our own will. He gives us free choice, but His desire is always to bless us. In the last verses of the Psalm, God tells how He wanted to bless Israel and deliver them from their enemies. *"He should have fed them all with the finest of the wheat: and with honey out of the rock should I have satisfied thee"* (v. 16).

If we want God's blessing, we need to give our will to Him and follow His principles and His plan for our life. Let's call on Him, do His will, and receive God's blessings on our life.

# ⚜Psalm 82

T HE PSALM starts with a statement about God: *"God standeth in the congregation of the mighty...."* But although the psalmist tells us God is mighty, he does not understand why God does not resolve certain issues. He asks why God does not defend and deliver the poor, the fatherless, and the needy. That question is the same one many people ask and often without receiving an answer. I have often wondered the same. I do not know the entire answer, but I do know a few truths.

I do know that the world is full of sin because man turned his back on God and disobeyed Him. Since Adam's sin, every person has been born with a sin nature. Trusting Christ as our Saviour will take care of our personal sin issue. But many people do not turn to God, which makes the world an evil place. Unfortunately, sin has consequences that cause troubles in the world.

I also know is that some people are not helped because they do not come to God. Verse five says, *"They know not, neither will they understand; they walk on in darkness."* They might not know because they refuse to think about God or allow Him in

174 | GERRI JOHNSON

their life. Or they might not know because Christians do not care enough to tell them. Jesus left us the Great Commission to tell us to preach the gospel to all nations, but we are often lax in fulfilling that responsibility. How sad that people could be delivered from their sins and problems, but we do not tell them about His saving power.

I know that *"without faith it is impossible to please him* [God]...." *And* I will never understand why everything happens, but I do not need to comprehend the mind of God. That God knows is enough. I only need to have faith that He does all things well. Although God allows man to make wrong choices, He is still in control. Verse eight says, *"Arise, O God, judge the earth: for thou shalt inherit all nations."* One day the Lord will reign over all. Evil doers will be punished, and we who have trusted in the Lord will live forever in a world made perfect.

Let's not worry if we do not understand why God allows certain things. Let's do our part to tell others about Christ, Who is the solution to the sin problem. Let's rejoice that one day we will live in a world ruled by Christ and free of sin and its multiple problems.

# ℘salm 83

ISRAEL'S ENEMIES were trying to destroy them, and the psalmist is pleading for God to destroy them. Looking at Israel as God's people and their enemies as Satan's hosts depicts the struggle seen all throughout History—good against evil. Of course, Israel was not perfect and often turned from God, but they were His chosen people, and He forgave them numerous times when they turned back to Him—just as He does for us when we falter and then turn back to Him.

Even as the psalmist asked for the destruction of their enemies, he also recorded in verse 16, *"Fill their faces with shame; that they may seek thy name, O LORD."* The psalmist desired for them to be saved if they would turn to God. But if they did not, he wanted God to defeat them. Verse 17 says, *"Let them be confounded and troubled for ever; yea, let them be put to shame, and perish."*

We face that same situation today. We are in a battle of good versus evil, and we should want good—God's side—to win. But although people are evil, we should first want their salvation. We should pray that all men would turn to God as individuals.

But we should also pray for victory for the forces of God. We want the enemy to be defeated, but want to reach as many as we can individually for the Lord.

Another reason the psalmist wanted God to judge the enemy is given in verse 18: *"That men may know that thou, whose name alone is JEHOVAH, art the most high over all the earth."* The psalmist was zealous for the name of the Lord. He wanted all to know the Lord's strength. Let's also be zealous for God's name, seek to serve the Lord, and reach people for Him. Let's show others how great God is and how He can make a difference in all of our lives.

# Psalm 84

BIRDS OFTEN build their nests in the strangest of places. Verse 3 says that the sparrows and swallows found a place to make their nest in God's house. The birds showed better sense than many of us! The first few verses of this Psalm list several characteristics about God's house.

**God's house is amiable** (v. 1). *Amiable* can mean "friendly" or "pleasant." We think of friendly as relating to people, and certainly the people in God's house should be friendly—not only to the regular members but also to visitors. Every person should feel the love of God. The synonym "pleasant" can also refer to people but can describe the place itself, although the people who attend God's house are the ones who make it pleasant. We should make visitors feel they are in a pleasant place.

**The psalmist longs to be in God's house** (v. 2). Because God should be most important in our life, we should want to be in His house. Yes, we can worship Him in nature or anywhere, but in His house we have fellowship with others who also love Him, as well as receive instruction from the preaching that we might not learn on our own.

**Those who make God's house an important part of their lives will receive His blessings.** Verse four says, *"Blessed are they that dwell in thy house: they will be still praising thee."* As He blesses us, we need to remember to praise Him!

The psalmist then mentions in verse 10b, *"I had rather be a doorkeeper in the house of my God, than to dwell in the tents of wickedness."* If we dwell with the wicked, we can perhaps accrue much of what the world seeks—fame, money, new houses and cars. But those are not lasting treasures. The psalmist knew where to put his values—in God and in the people of God.

Let's desire to be in God's house and strive to make it a friendly place. Let's walk uprightly in His house and allow God to bless us. Let's make the house of God of utmost importance in our life, wanting God's house and His people in our life more than the fleeting treasures of this world.

# Psalm 85

HAVE YOU ever felt unhappy with yourself or depressed about how you see yourself? At times I have felt I was the worst mother, wife, and Christian! These feelings often arise when we are not as close to God as we should be.

Verse six says, *"Wilt thou not revive us again: that thy people may rejoice in thee?"* The psalmist is asking for the nation of Israel to experience revival as a whole, but each individual needs to seek that personal revival when his joy in the Lord seems to have gone.

Verse ten links mercy and truth together. We need reviving when we have stopped walking completely in God's truth, but He always has mercy (compassion, forgiveness) when we have wandered from the way.

Righteousness and peace are also linked together in that verse. God is righteous, but we often seem to turn from His way. When we turn back to Him, He gives us peace again in our hearts.

Verse 13 says, *"Righteousness shall go before him; and shall set us in the way of his steps."* When we seek His righteousness and live a life of integrity following Him, then He will set us in the way we should go. Let's follow in His steps, live righteously, and allow Him to do the work of reviving our hearts and giving us peace.

# $\mathfrak{P}$salm 86

$I$N VERSE one, the psalmist states he is poor and needy—the state of all of us before we come to Christ. Verse five states, *"For thou, Lord, art good, and ready to forgive; and plenteous in mercy unto all them that call upon thee."*

Have you ever held a grudge? Someone does something to you that you don't like, and you don't want to forgive the person—even if he or she asks for forgiveness. We often harbor issues in our heart against others. Thankfully, God, Who would have every reason to hold a grudge, does not. He is good and always ready to forgive us when we sin. Of course, we should want to do right, but when we fail, He is always ready to forgive us and has plenty of mercy.

*Mercy* is "compassion or forgiveness to someone you have the power to punish." God certainly has the power and right to punish us, and sometimes He does correct us if we continue in our wrongdoing. God corrects us in love and always wants to bring us back into fellowship with Him.

Verse 15 gives some characteristics about our God. *"But thou, O Lord, art a God full of compassion, and gracious, long-*

*suffering, and plenteous in mercy and truth."* We can see God's compassion in His readiness to forgive and bring us back to Himself. *Grace* is "unmerited favor." We certainly do not merit God's goodness to us, but He constantly offers it.

*Longsuffering* is exactly what it says—suffering long—referring to "having patience in spite of trouble," especially when that trouble is caused by other people. If God's patience can be tried, I am certain we try His patience as we frequently live our up-and-down lives. We trust Him and serve Him, and then our faith fails or we turn from Him because He has allowed some pain in our life.

But God has plenty of mercy and truth. He shows His mercy each time we turn back to Him. We need to fill ourselves with His truth, which we find His Word. Jesus Himself used Scripture against the Devil. How much more do we need to study and learn it to have a defense against Satan?

Let's say with the psalmist, *"Teach me thy way, O LORD; I will walk in thy truth..."* (v. 11).

# Psalm 87

WE SOMETIMES like to brag about where we are from. When attending a meeting or a conference, the delegates are often asked where they are from. When the attendees respond, cheers are often heard from the other delegates when their particular state is mentioned.

Verse five says, *"And of Zion it shall be said, This and that man was born in her."* If a conference convened in the Holy Land and the name *Jerusalem* were mentioned, the applause would have been thunderous. *"The LORD loveth the gates of Zion more than all the dwellings of Jacob. Glorious things are spoken of thee, O city of God"* (vv. 2, 3). Zion, or Jerusalem, the capital of the land God gave His chosen people, was a special place to God.

Most of the history of Israel revolves around Jerusalem, the place where Israel's kings reigned and where many New Testament events happened. Although Jesus was not born in Zion, many events of His life happened in this special place.

I studied in the Holy Land during one semester in college and lived on the Mount of Olives. Taking a walk into the old city was easy and fascinating; seeing the historical sights of Golgotha (Calvary), the garden tomb, and possible sites of where Jesus was crucified and buried was thrilling. I don't know why God chose Jerusalem as His special city, but I can understand why He loved Zion. My dream is to return someday.

What is important is to love the Word of God that describes the events that happened there, to love the God Who chose that place as His special place, and to share with others about the Lord Who was crucified, buried, and resurrected there so that we could have salvation.

Let's make the God Who chose Israel as His special people and Jerusalem as His special city our God. Let's serve Him and share His gospel message with others. Let's be proud to be counted as His people.

# 𝕻salm 88

I N THIS entire Psalm the author is telling how he is cast down and afflicted. In verse four he describes himself *as a man that hath no strength.* Physically, I know the feeling of having no strength. Usually I am fairly healthy, but as I write this chapter, I am getting over being sick. I had to walk up some stairs to where my computer is, and I held on to the railing and paused every two steps. I felt weak and without strength. Feeling that way is no fun.

The psalmist, though, is talking about spiritual strength. Any number of issues could cause our spiritual weakness. God's Word tells us what we need in order to be strong spiritually: God's Word, prayer, the Holy Spirit, and the church.

1) **The Bible is God's way of speaking to us.** We need it to learn His principles to guide us in living our life.

2) **Prayer is our talking to God.** We can take our requests and praises to Him. You would not think of going a long time without speaking to someone you love, whether a spouse, children, other family members, or friends. How can we go long periods of time without talking to our God and Saviour?

3) **God gave us the Holy Spirit to abide in us to be a consoler and instructor in His Word.** He also "gets on our case" when we do something that displeases Him.

4) **The church is where we can fellowship with other believers.** From fellow believers we receive strength and encouragement, and we also hear messages from the pastor that can help increase our understanding of Scripture.

We need to take advantage of all four to gain spiritual strength and to avoid losing it. Let's read our Bible, pray, allow the Holy Spirit to direct us, and be faithful in church to maintain our spiritual strength.

# $\mathfrak{P}$salm 89

"*I WILL SING of the mercies of the* LORD *for ever: with my mouth will I make known thy faithfulness to all generations*" (v. 1). The psalmist says he will sing of God's mercies forever, and really, we could all go on singing, praising, and telling of God's mercies without end. First, He saved us. Then, He forgives us every time we fail Him, when we come to Him confessing our fault. We can also be assured of His mercies in the future. Verse two says His mercy shall be built up forever. He will always be merciful, no matter how many times we fail Him.

The psalmist also says he will tell of God's faithfulness to all generations. We should always be ready to tell of God's faithfulness to us. Man disappoints us and fails us, but God never does. In verse two the psalmist says that God's faithfulness is established in the heavens. Every year, every decade, every century, every millennium, the world continues in its rhythms because God controls it and faithfully watches over His creation. Night follows day. Spring, summer, fall, and winter follow each other continuously. The sun, moon, planets, and heavenly bodies are held in their courses by the faithfulness of God.

If God established the heavens and keeps them in their pre-scribed courses, how much more is He faithful to watch over us? Verse five says, *"And the heavens shall praise thy wonders, O LORD: thy faithfulness also in the congregation of the saints."* The next two verses say no one can compare to the Lord and He should be feared and reverenced. We need to fear God in the sense of being awed with His greatness, and because of that awe, want to serve Him. We also need to reverence Him. Reverence involves great respect, acclaim, and admiration.

Verse 52 ends the Psalm saying, *"Blessed be the LORD for evermore...."* Let's bless Him and sing and tell of God's mercies and faithfulness, praising Him for what He does in our lives. With respect and admiration, let's tell of His goodness to us.

# 𝔓salm 90

THIS PSALM shows how fleeting time is—1,000 years are as a day (v. 4). *"In the morning they are like grass which groweth up. In the morning it flourisheth, and groweth up; in the evening it is cut down and withereth"* (vv. 5a, 6).

Realizing how quickly time passes, every child of God should consider two truths:

*1) We need to make right our relationship with God.* So many people want to enjoy life on their terms and then plan to settle things with God when they are old. But we are not assured that we will even live to old age. Others accept the Lord as Saviour but then are not concerned with really serving Him. They might have pleasures and sins they want to continue enjoying.

But verse eight says, *"Thou hast set our iniquities before thee, our secret sins in the light of thy countenance."* We cannot hide anything from God. We also do not know how much time we have here on earth. Let's make sure we have confessed our sins and received His salvation. Then let's keep our lives free from secret sins, daily examining our lives and keeping them right with our God.

---

Verse 14 says, *"O satisfy us early with thy mercy; that we may rejoice and be glad all our days."* Why waste the limited time we have here on earth? If we give our lives to Him early, we can have His joy with us all our days. That leads us to the second truth in regard to the swift passing of time.

2) **Once our sin issue is cared for, we should want to use every moment for good.** Verse 12 says, *"So teach us to number our days, that we may apply our hearts unto wisdom."* So many times we just let our day "happen." We do not plan what to do, and so often we waste many minutes and hours, which can add up to years not taken advantage of in our lives.

Verse 17 says, *"And let the beauty of the LORD our God be upon us: and establish thou the work of our hands upon us."* Let's not waste our time, but seek God's wisdom and let God's beauty be seen in us as we do the work He has for us in our lives.

# Psalm 91

"HE that dwelleth in the secret place of the most high shall abide under the shadow of the Almighty." The mighty promise of verse one is beautiful! Sometimes we do not like the darkness of shadows. As a child, did you ever get scared and have trouble sleeping because you saw a shadow in the closet or in a corner of the room? Weren't you absolutely sure someone was lurking there? Indeed, shadows can be scary. But a shadow also reveals that something is there, and if we are under the shadow of the Almighty, He is covering us, which is a comforting thought rather than a frightful one.

But who is under His shadow? It is the one who is dwelling in His secret place. I think of His secret place as that place of daily fellowship with Him. The New Testament tells us to pray in secret, rather than for all to see. And when we set apart time each day to read our Bible and pray, we are coming to Him "secretly"—alone and without anything else distracting us. When we have the habit of doing that, we are in His secret place, and He holds us close under His shadow.

Verses five and six give us four specific situations in which we are protected and should not fear. We should not be afraid of the following situations:

*"For the terror by night."* We don't have to fear that shadow in the closet or any other thing lurking in the darkness. Darkness can bring fear, but we are safe under God's wings.

*"Nor for the arrow that flieth by day."* We may not have literal arrows flying at us, but we will face enemies in our life, especially Satan and anything He may throw our way. But God is with us, so we already have the victory.

*"Nor for the pestilence that walketh in darkness."* Once again, we have darkness, but God is our light. Whether pestilence refers to disease or any horrible trial, God is with us in the dark days of our lives.

*"Nor for the destruction that wasteth at noonday."* Even in broad daylight, things can come in our life that threaten to destroy us. God is there to give deliverance—if we trust Him.

Let's spend time in His secret place. Let's rest under the shadow of His wings in every situation in which we may find ourselves.

# $\mathfrak{P}$salm 92

THIS PSALM begins by telling the reader that giving thanks to the Lord and showing His lovingkindness and faithfulness is good. These characteristics that God shows toward them that love Him are certainly wonderful, and we should surely share them with others.

The psalmist then states how great God and His works are. But verse six tells of two kinds of people who cannot see this truth.

• **The brutish man.** The word *brutish,* which seems to describe many people today, can mean "cruel or unkind" or "lacking intelligence." To me, this second definition really describes many people who are intelligent in their own eyes, and in the eyes of the world, but who will not believe in a loving, caring God.

• **The fool, or the unwise person.** Anyone who does not accept the lovingkindness of God in his or her life is certainly unwise.

Verse seven tells us of their end: *"When the wicked spring as the grass, and when all the workers of iniquity do flourish; it*

*is that they shall be destroyed for ever."* How sad it is to think
of that day! This ending is why we need to share God's lovingkindness and faithfulness with others.

The righteous, on the other hand, are described in verse
12: *"The righteous shall flourish like the palm tree: he shall grow
like a cedar in Lebanon."* What a contrast the palm tree is to the
grass! The tall, flowing palm trees are lovely to see. They sway
in the wind rather than being broken by the storms of life. The
cedar of Lebanon is a huge tree that was much valued for its
wood in Bible times.

But our soil is not the dirt we find outside. Verse 13 says,
*"Those that be planted in the house of the LORD shall flourish in
the courts of our God."* How much time do we spend in God's
house? Do we only attend at Christmas and Easter as some do?
Or are we there regularly, firmly planted?

Let's put our roots down deep in God's house, and let's con-
sistently tell others of God's lovingkindness, faithfulness, and
salvation so they can likewise be rooted in Him.

# ℘salm 93

THIS FAIRLY short Psalm begins with telling us three facts about the Lord in the first verse: He reigns, He is clothed with majesty, and He is clothed with strength.

**He reigns.** Over what does the Lord reign? He could reign over this world, but He turned over His right to Satan, whom He calls the Prince of the Power of the Air. But Satan will rule only temporarily. He is coming back to reign on this earth for one thousand years in a time of peace when Satan is bound, and then He will make a new heaven and earth. Satan will be judged as well as all those who would not accept Christ and let Him reign in their lives. Then the Lord will reign forever over a perfect kingdom. How wonderful that will be!

Christ does not currently reign over the world, but He does reign in the hearts of those who have accepted His gift of salvation.

**He is clothed with majesty.** The word *majesty* is "sovereign power or greatness." One day that sovereign power will be seen as He reigns over all of His creation in greatness. But until then, since He reigns in our hearts, we need to allow Him to use His sovereignty in our lives. He knows all things, and letting Him be in control, instead of wanting our own will, is best.

**He is clothed with strength.** As we allow Him to reign in and control our lives, He will give us the strength to have victory over our enemies and over troubles and difficulties in our life.

His strength is also seen in creation. Verse one concludes, *"the world also is stablished, that it cannot be moved."* He hung the heavenly bodies in place, and His strength holds them there. Some stars may fall, but the universe is controlled by Him and will not be moved as a whole until He forms a new heaven and a new earth for us and rids the world of sin and its debilitating effects.

The last verse of this Psalm tells us His testimonies are sure. We can trust what His Word says. We can rest in the fact that He will reign forever. The final verse concludes this Psalm with *"holiness becometh thine house, O LORD, for ever."* We are part of His house when we know Him as Saviour. Let's strive to keep ourselves holy for Him.

# Psalm 94

Verse three cites the ever-present question: "*Lord, how long shall the wicked, how long shall the wicked triumph?*" The psalmist asked this question over and over, and His children often ask it today. The wicked seemingly always have everything, and those who serve God and try to do right, following His principles, often have so little of what the world thinks important—fame, monetary assets, and material goods.

Verses seven and nine show us what the wicked think, as well as what reality is. The wicked say in verse seven, "*The Lord shall not see,*" but the psalmist asserts in verse nine, "*he that formed the eye, shall he not see?*" Verse 11 assures us that God knows that the thoughts of men are vanity. We may think the wicked are "getting away with things," but God sees. In His time and in His way, He will bring justice.

In verse 16, the psalmist asks who will rise up for him against the evildoers and tells us in verses 17 and 18, "*Unless the Lord had been my help, my soul had almost dwelt in silence. When I said, My foot slippeth; thy mercy, O Lord held me up.*" We have that same help available to us today. When we feel discouraged because of the wicked, the Lord is always there to hold us up.

The psalmist may have struggled with negative thoughts when He saw injustice and the wicked seeming to win over the righteous. But in verse 19 we see the psalmist's secret for victory: *"In the multitude of my thoughts within me thy comforts delight my soul."*

Instead of focusing His thoughts on the wicked and the seeming injustice, the psalmist turned his thoughts inward. Perhaps he thought of the joy His salvation brought or the peace we have in Christ. Perhaps he thought about the wonderful attributes of our God—His love, mercy, and kindness. He allowed those thoughts to delight His soul. Let's keep our thoughts positive. Let's not focus on the wicked and the world around us. Let's instead look inside at all the Lord has done for us and, like the psalmist, let His comforts delight our soul.

# Psalm 95

VERSE TWO says, *"Let us come before his presence with thanksgiving, and make a joyful noise unto him with psalms."* The Psalms comprised the hymnbook of the Jewish people. We are to come to God in song, and thankfully, that singing only has to make a joyful noise—not necessarily be a good voice!

When we are excited about some matter, don't we often feel our excitement almost bubbling out of us? That is how I picture coming when we come to Him in thanksgiving for all He has done. Four reasons are mentioned in this wonderful Psalm for which we can praise God.

**He is a great God and great King above all gods** (v. 3). Most religions worship a man who has died. Our Lord died but rose from the dead. He is great and all-powerful. Let's be sure to praise Him for His greatness.

**He is a Creator** (vv. 4, 5). He made and controls the deep places, the hills, the sea, and the dry land. He is our maker, and thus verse 6 says to bow down and kneel before Him. Our God deserves our reverence and praise.

**He is our Shepherd, and we are His sheep (v. 7).** When we accept Him as our Saviour, He becomes our Shepherd and we are the people of His pasture. Jesus also used this imagery to describe our relationship to Him in the New Testament. What a beautiful relationship of a loving shepherd caring for and leading His sheep! We should praise our God for His care for us.

**He is the rock of our salvation (v. 1).** Not only is He our Saviour, but He is our Rock—our firm foundation upon Whom to build our lives. In an unstable world, that foundation should be something for which to praise the Lord.

So, for these and many other reasons, let's make a joyful noise unto Him!

# Psalm 96

IN VERSES one and two, God's people are instructed to *"sing unto the* LORD." Many times when someone is happy, that person will hum, whistle, or sing as he walks or goes about his activities. Singing is a natural part of life, and if we are joyful because of what God has done in our lives, we should express that delight in song. I am not referring to singing a solo in church (unless you have a great voice and can use this talent for the Lord). Rather, I am alluding to expressing your joy in song—perhaps singing and rejoicing in the shower or singing along with a song you are listening to.

Verse two then instructs us to *"bless his name."* To do so, we need to think about all that He has done for us. Indeed, we should have a huge list for which to bless and praise Him. So bless His name, perhaps telling someone one-on-one about how He has blessed you or sharing a testimony about a specific blessing.

Verse two also tells the child of God to *"shew forth his salvation from day to day."* If we are saved, we should be sharing that good news with other people. Too many times we are too

202 | GERRI JOHNSON

afraid or embarrassed to tell someone else about our faith. But we should be looking for opportunities each day to share God's plan of salvation with someone. If people do not hear this good news from us, they may not hear about God's love and desire to save from any other source.

Verse three continues along this same line. *"Declare his glory among the heathen, his wonders among all people."* One way to be a witness is to share all that God has done for us—with everyone. We need to be "soul conscious"—constantly aware that those around us have a soul that will spend eternity in heaven or hell.

Let's sing unto the Lord and bless His name. Let's especially keep our eyes open for times we can share His salvation and His wonders with others.

# Psalm 97

VERSE TEN says, *"Ye that love the LORD, hate evil...."* This verse shows the comparison of opposites: love and hate, the Lord and evil. If we love the Lord, logic would dictate that we would hate evil. But that logic does not seem to be true in the life of many a believer.

Some Christians love the fact that they are saved and thus on their way to heaven, but they still want to dabble a little in the world. They are not ready to give up some things in their lives to serve the Lord fully. They are glad to be saved—but not ready to hate evil and rid themselves of everything unholy in their lives. The psalmist admonishes us to hate evil if we love the Lord.

Perhaps if we reflected more on the remainder of verse ten, we would be more ready to hate evil. Referencing the Lord's working in our lives, the verse states, *"he preserveth the souls of his saints: he delivereth them out of the hand of the wicked."* Because He preserves our soul, Satan can no longer harm us. Then He delivers us from the hand of the wicked. The world can do nothing to us that God does not allow. If we meditated more on these truths, perhaps we would be more ready to purge any wrong thing from our life and really hate evil because God hates it.

Verse 11 tells us God gives light to the righteous and gladness to the upright in heart. As we hate evil and thus live righteously, God's light guides us. As we live uprightly, our hearts are filled with gladness.

As He fills us with gladness, we can do as the psalmist says in verse 12: *"Rejoice in the LORD, ye righteous; and give thanks at the remembrance of his holiness."*

Let's love God, hate evil, and rejoice in our hearts as we remember His holiness.

# ℙsalm 98

Have you ever been anxious to know how a story ends, so you turned to the last chapter to see what happens before you had read the entire story? You simply wanted to know that the happy ending you hoped for truly happens! And if a villain is present, you want to know that he is punished.

The Bible has recorded a happy ending for this world. At least, the ending is a happy one for the righteous—for those who know the Lord as their Saviour. The end will be unhappy for the unrighteous and God's enemies. The end of this Psalm gives us a glimpse of that ending—God's judging the world in righteousness. The psalmist even tells nature, as well as man, to rejoice: *"Let the sea roar, and the fulness thereof; the world, and they that dwell therein. Let the floods clap their hands: let the hills be joyful together"* (vv. 7, 8).

The end will be a happy time, and because we already know the ending, we can rejoice and be thankful now. So in this Psalm, we are reminded to sing a new song and make a joyful noise unto the Lord.

We are also reminded that God has done marvelous things

and of His wonderful salvation, mercy, and truth. Let's remember what God has done, and until the last chapters unfold, let's sing and make a joyful noise unto the Lord!

# Psalm 99

GOD is described as holy in three verses of this Psalm (vv. 3, 5, 9). *Holy* means "exalted, worthy of complete devotion, or perfect in goodness and righteousness." Because God is holy, we are told to exalt, worship, and praise Him.

Since God is in an exalted position, we should exalt Him in our lives. We need to see Him in His uplifted position and lift Him up in our lives by making Him Lord and giving Him first place in our lives.

Because God is worthy of complete devotion, we should worship Him. *Worship* is "showing reverence and adoration for a deity." When we *reverence* God, we show our deference to Him, wanting Him to control our lives. *Adoration* shows our attitude toward God, realizing He is above all. Verse five instructs the child of God to *"worship at his footstool,"* which shows our complete subjection to Him.

Because God is perfect in goodness and righteousness, we should praise Him. As we reflect on the attributes of God, we should find praising Him easy.

Starting in verse six, we see how our holy God interacted

with men of the past—Moses, Aaron, and Samuel. These men called upon God and also kept His testimonies and ordinances. God responded in three ways.

1) **God answered them.** When we pray to God, He hears us and answers us. Sometimes the answer is not immediate, but if we are faithful in prayer, He always hears and answers.

2) **God forgave them.** Although these were men of God, they were not perfect. We also sin and make mistakes, but when we come to the Lord, thankfully He is always ready to forgive us and restore our fellowship with Him.

3) **God took vengeance on their "inventions."** He forgave them, and He forgives us, but because He is holy, we still suffer the consequences for our sin.

Let's remember that God is holy, and let us seek to exalt, worship, and praise Him.

# Psalm 100

*I* WANT TO share a few thoughts from each verse of this fairly short Psalm.

Verse one commands us to make a joyful noise to the Lord. It doesn't matter if we are talented musically or have a beautiful voice, God wants us to express our praise to Him. The verse ends with *"all ye lands."* Everyone is to worship and praise God. No one is an exception. He wants all people to come to Him.

Verse two repeats the command to come to God with singing and also instructs His people to serve Him with gladness. Unfortunately, some people don't seem to want to serve Him at all. They are satisfied that they are on their way to heaven but do not want to take any responsibility to serve. Others may serve in their local church but do not serve with gladness. They consider their service to be more of an obligation than a benefit. God wants us to be glad in our service to Him.

Verse three reminds us that the Lord is God and that He made us, which gives us a responsibility to serve Him. The verse then compares us to His sheep. We are helpless without

Him, but as a shepherd cares for his sheep, the Lord wants to care for and lead us.

Verse four tells us to enter His house with thanksgiving and with praise. Some Christians do not even seem to want to enter His house. They prefer to follow their own desires. The Lord's day becomes a day to sleep in, take a joy ride, or visit family or friends. Our desire and priority should be to attend church when the doors are open. When we go, we should go with a heart of thanksgiving for all of the blessings He has bestowed upon us during the week and with praise in our hearts and mouths.

Verse five reminds us that God is good. We end every service at our church with the phrase, "God is good all the time; all the time God is good." What an excellent reminder of His goodness and the importance of reflecting on it throughout the week.

Let's remember that God IS good and that He made us. Because of this, let's be faithful in His house and give Him praise with thanksgiving.

# 𝔓salm 101

𝕴N VERSE one the psalmist says He will sing of mercy and judgment. I am so glad that with God mercy and judgment walk hand-in-hand. We all are sinners and deserve the judgment of God. Without God's mercy, there would be no hope for us. But in His mercy, He provided a way for our salvation through what Jesus did for us on the cross. Even after we accept His gift of salvation, we often fail Him. But over and over He extends His mercy to us to bring us back into His fellowship.

In verses two and three, the psalmist mentions three decisions He is determined to enact in His life.

1) *"I will behave myself wisely in a perfect way"* (v. 2a). *Wisely* means in a way that shows experience, knowledge, and good judgment. Experience can only be gathered over time, but the best way to have the right experiences is to make our lives revolve around the church.

The most important knowledge is that which we acquire by spending time in God's Word, the means to develop good judgment—by studying God's judgments and principles. Psalm 119:30 says, *"I have chosen the way of truth: thy judgments have*

*I laid before me."* Verse 106 says, *"I have sworn, and I will per-
form it, that I will keep thy righteous judgments."*

2) *"I will walk within my house with a perfect heart"* (v.
2b). How many times have you heard people say the church is
full of hypocrites? Sadly, their accusation is often true. Christians act very religious and holy at church, but the "proof" of
their faith is often found at home. How do we act behind closed
doors with our family? Do we live out God's principles there? Is
our heart perfect in our daily living with our family?

3) *"I will set no wicked thing before mine eyes"* (v. 3a). In
today's world, we are bombarded by the wrong visual images
on every side. With huge unbecoming billboards posted everywhere, people scandalously dressed in public, and indecency
and immorality shown on television and video, completely
protecting our eyes from seeing something inappropriate is
next to impossible. But we can decide whether we will continue to look at that which is inappropriate. Immediately turn
your eyes from wickedness. Don't watch television programs
that are not wholesome and immediately turn off an inappropriate commercial.

Let's be wise, live righteously at home, and carefully guard
our eyes from evil!

# Psalm 102

VERSE 11 says, *"My days are like a shadow that declineth; and I am withered like grass."* When the sun comes up in the morning, it gets higher and higher until midday, then lower and lower until sunset. The shadows become weaker as evening approaches. The psalmist compares his life to the weakening shadow, as we often have less strength as we get older. He also says he is withered like the grass. I can identify with that description. I hope the Lord gives me many more years, but I am well past midday in my life! I have less strength, but what I notice most is my skin "withering" and becoming wrinkly.

Many women don't tell their age, but telling my age has never been an issue for me—maybe because I always looked younger than my actual age. But I do not like the fact that now I am not even asked if I am a senior citizen! I guess it must be obvious with one look at the wrinkles on my face and my flabby arms.

We all know we have only so much time on this earth, although we do not know exactly how much. We need to decide to make every moment count for God. Are we spending all of our time seeking our own pleasures, or are we seeking to serve the Lord with the time He has given us?

Our reflection on the message of verse 11 should cause us to realize we have little time and prompt us to use the time we have to serve the Lord.

Verse 12 paints the opposite picture: *"But thou, O LORD shalt endure for ever."* Verse 27 adds, *"But thou art the same, and thy years shall have no end."* We are finite beings, but God who loves us is eternal. I think we spend too little time reflecting on Who and what God is and praising Him for His attributes. He is from everlasting to everlasting. We cannot begin to fathom that attribute, but we can praise Him for it. He also does not change. He loved us even before He created us and will love us with the same love throughout our lives and into eternity, where He has prepared a place for us. He never changes.

Let's praise Him for Who He is.

# Psalm 103

WE ARE told in this Psalm to bless the Lord. I think sometimes we have a very vague idea of what that means. How do we bless God? Synonyms for *bless* include "praise, worship, glorify, honor, exalt, adore"—all tangible actions that we can put into practice. We are to bless Him and not forget His benefits.

Verses three through five show five benefits God bestows upon us:

1) **He forgives our sins.** His forgiveness is the biggest benefit because without our sins' being forgiven, we cannot enter into heaven.

2) **He heals our diseases.** The gift of healing does not exist today. Individual men do not have power to heal whomever they want whenever they want. But God still heals. He tells us to pray and ask Him for healing. He may have a purpose for illness at times in our lives, but we should still pray for healing for ourselves and for others.

3) **He redeems us from destruction.** We are redeemed from hell when we trust Him as our Saviour, but He wants to

keep us from destruction in our lives now. We can make a mess of our lives doing things in our own will, but if we ask for help and want to follow His will, He wants to guide us.

4) **He shows His lovingkindness and tender mercies.** As we submit our lives to Him, He wraps His love and kindness around us. His mercy was shown when He saved us, but I like to think of "tender" mercies as the small ways He shows mercy to us on a daily basis.

5) **He fills our mouth with good things.** I like to think of this benefit as both literal and figurative. He supplies the food we need—many times with favorites that delight us. We have had some times of meagerness, but even then we at least had rice to eat. At other times, He provided a special desire. But He gives us more than just our food, He gives us many good things in our lives. We often take them for granted, but they all are blessings from God.

Let's bless God for all His benefits toward us!

# ℘salm 104

THIS PSALM uses beautiful poetic language to describe God's creation. Verse one tells us that the Lord God is very great. That greatness is revealed in verse five, which says He laid the foundations of the earth, and the Psalm goes on to describe what happened during the creation week. The foundations were covered with water, and then God caused the water to recede, forming mountains and valleys and seas and lakes.

Then He talks about the animals and birds, as well as all the vegetation God caused to grow as provision and beauty for man and animal. Verse 14 says, *"He causeth the grass to grow for the cattle, and herb for the service of man."* He had everything intricately planned and gave both beast and man exactly what they needed.

Verse 19 says, *"He appointed the moon for seasons: the sun knoweth his going down."* Nature knows what it is supposed to do. What a lesson that should be for us! Sadly, man often does not care about God's plan. To summarize, verse 24 says, *"O LORD, how manifold are thy works! In wisdom hast thou made them all: the earth is full of thy riches."*

The psalmist then adds more about the great sea. The creatures that live in the sea are amazing and often strange! Some fish even are fluorescent, and the psalmist says in verse 27: *"These wait all upon thee: that thou mayest give them their meat in due season."* These sea creatures have more sense than many humans, who do not trust God to supply their needs and instead live in constant frustration.

The psalmist ends the chapter with two concluding thoughts: **He will sing to and praise God as long as He lives** (v. 33). That attitude should also be ours as we look at God's marvelous creation and His provisions for us.

**He will meditate on all God had done.** *"My meditation of him shall be sweet: I will be glad in the LORD"* (v. 34). We need to be amazed at creation and praise God but also really take time to meditate on all He has done. Let's meditate on His creation and say like the psalmist, *"I will be glad in the LORD"* (v. 34).

# Psalm 105

Verse one tells us three things we should do: *"O give thanks unto the Lord; call upon his name: make known his deeds among the people."*

**Give thanks.**

Just the fact that we wake up in the morning is a reason to give thanks. He has given us one more day of life, and during that day, He will provide us with air to breath. He gave us the strength to provide for our clothing, housing, and food. He gives us many other blessing throughout our days.

**Call upon Him.**

But problems and difficulties come that leave us not knowing what to do. What we should do is call upon Him. Unfortunately, seeking Him is usually the last choice—after all of our other options have failed. But we need to call on His name to help us and make intercession for others.

**Make His deeds known.**

Then God wants us to make His deeds known. The following verses cite all of the things God did for the nation of Israel, starting with Abraham, then mentioning Joseph, Moses, the plagues, the exodus, God's provision in the wilderness, and the arrival of the children of Israel in the Promised Land.

We may not be part of the nation of Israel, but God does wonderful deeds for us too, and verse two tells us to tell people about our blessings from God. *"Talk ye of all his wondrous works"* (v. 2b). What has God done for you in your personal life that you can share with others?

Let's do as the psalmist instructed the Israelites. Let's thank Him, call upon Him, and share His blessings in our lives.

# ℘salm 106

THIS PSALM recounts how God delivered the Israelites at the Red Sea, leading them across on dry ground and then destroying the enemy. Verse 12 says, *"Then believed they his words; they sang his praise."*

I find it so sad that verse 12 begins with *"then."* We are just like the people of Israel at that time. We don't really believe God will act and help us until we see His hand work in great strength. When we see Him do something great for us, **then** we believe Him and praise Him. We only have to "see it to believe it." After we see proof of what He can do, **then** we praise Him and perhaps trust Him for a while.

The next verse exposes the reaction of Israel soon after that miracle in their lives: *"They soon forgat his works; they waited not for his counsel"* (v. 13). I used to find it amazing how many times God performed a marvelous work for His people in their journey from Egypt to the Promised Land, only to see them soon doubting God again. But the longer I live, the more I realize we are just like the Israelites. We murmur and complain when He does not help us when we want and in the way we want.

---

Verse 15 shares the sad conclusion to the situation, *"And he gave them their request; but sent leanness into their soul."* They got what they asked for, but without spiritual fullness—without God's peace and joy.

Do you sometimes pray, but you are praying for God to answer your request or solve the problem the way **you** want things to turn out? Have you ever received something you asked for but afterward still did not have peace or joy?

God knows best what we need. We should pray for God's help, but with the attitude of wanting whatever answer He sees best. Sometimes He has a plan much better that what we had imagined. When we allow Him to answer in the way He knows best, His answer will be accompanied by peace and joy.

Let's believe God will answer our prayers, praise Him when He does, and bask in the peace and joy He brings.

# Psalm 107

IF SOMETHING is mentioned more than once in the Bible, we can trust that God considers it important. One statement is quoted four times in this Psalm: *"Oh that men would praise the LORD for his goodness, and for his wonderful works to the children of men!"* (vv. 8, 15, 21, 31). Each time the verse ends with an exclamation mark. I would say that God is placing emphasis on the truth stated.

We are told four times to praise God for His goodness and His wonderful works. In other words, we should praise God for who He is and for what He does. Do we take the time to reflect on His goodness and His wonderful works and consciously thank Him and praise Him?

I find it interesting that in the verses before each of these repeated verses, man is in some state of wandering from or rebellion to God. Finally, in each case, they cried unto the Lord in their trouble, and God delivered them. Do we have to wait until we are in trouble to turn our attention to God?

This interesting cycle seems to repeat over and over with Israel and continues with all men even until today. When life goes well, we tend to forget about God. Oh, we may stay faithful in church and with our Christian activities, but we don't have that fervent rejoicing in Who God is and what He does for us.

Then when difficulties come and we don't seem to be able to resolve things on our own, we remember God and call on Him for help. He helps us because He always loves us.

Let's learn from this constant cycle so that we can reflect, like the psalmist says in the last verse: *"Whoso is wise, and will observe these things, even they shall understand the lovingkindness of the LORD."*

# ℜsalm 108

VERSE 12 SAYS, *"Give us help from trouble: for vain is the help of man."* The only place to receive real help from our problems is from God. This verse tells us that man's help is vain. I found two definitions for the word *vain* that I want to mention.

The first definition is "useless." If we realize that man's help is really useless, then we will immediately come to God to resolve our problems and difficulties. That is the best action to take. God is always ready to help us when we come to Him.

The second definition is "not yielding the desired outcome." Too many people decide to try to get their help from worldly sources. They may turn to friends, worldly counsel, or any source other than God. I am not saying we should never seek counsel. God can use the advice of godly people to help us in some situations, but our confidence should be in God rather than in people.

But many will turn anywhere rather than to God. When things do not work out as they expected or hoped and they do not get the desired result, then they will turn to God. They wasted time and possibly suffered heartache before finally turning to the One Who can truly help them.

Verse 13, *"Through God we shall do valiantly: for he it is that shall tread down our enemies."* *Valiantly* means "with courage or determination." *Courage* means "the ability to do something that frightens us." We often have the mistaken idea that if we are courageous, we will be without fear. That thought is not true. *Courage* means "we will act in spite of our fear." So when we trust in God, He gives us the power to act in spite of fear.

Another definition of *courage* is "strength in the face of pain or grief." Perhaps we are not fearing the outcome of a situation but are facing an illness or loss. God can give strength to face those situations and get through them. He does not take away the difficulty but walks with us through it and gives us grace and strength.

Let's seek God's help first in every situation and lean on Him for the strength to be victorious.

# ℙsalm 109

IN THIS Psalm the psalmist asks God for vengeance and judgment on His enemies. At times He makes this same request in other Psalms, and I will admit, I do not know how to react to his desire. Are there times when God allows us to wish vengeance on our enemies or those who treat us wrongly?

I am not sure of the answer, but I do know two facts about the psalmist's situation that make me believe He acted correctly. He had been treated hatefully. *"They compassed me about also with words of hatred; and fought against me without a cause"* (v. 3). But His actions and attitudes were not retaliatory or vindictive. *"For my love they are my adversaries: but I give myself unto prayer. And they have rewarded me evil for good and hatred for my love"* (vv. 4, 5).

Although his enemies still continued to hate Him, He still did not retaliate. Instead, he prayed because he knew prayer can resolve many issues.

Although the psalmist's enemies did not become his friends or allies, he made the decision to ask God to take vengeance, rather than trying to do it himself. Verse 27 says, *"That they may know that this is thy hand.*" He wanted revenge, but He left matters with God.

How easy it is for us, also, to wish bad on those who have hurt us. We need to remember to take the correct steps that the psalmist took. First, let's show love and do good to our enemies. Second, let's pray about the situation. We should pray for God to work both in our enemy's life and in our own. Third, let's leave it in God's hand to execute vengeance if He so wishes. Whatever the result, let's say as the psalmist in verse 30, *"I will greatly praise the LORD with my mouth; yea, I will praise him among the multitude."*

# Psalm 110

"T HE LORD *said unto my Lord, Sit thou at my right hand until I make thine enemies thy footstool.*" A *footstool* is place of low esteem because it is only a rest for the feet. In this Psalm, God the Father is talking to God the Son, telling Him His enemies will become like a footstool. He will put His feet on them in victory.

Today, because God in His eternal plan allows it, Satan is currently the prince of this world—but not for always. This Psalm tells us how Jesus will come in power and destroy the Enemy, judge the heathen, and rule over all. What a wonderful time that will be when we look to Jesus as our leader!

Verse four also mentions the order of the priest Melchizedek, Who is Jesus. In the Old Testament, the priest served as the go-between for God and man. Because Jesus became the supreme sacrifice for our sin, He is now our priest, and we have no need for any man to serve as a mediator between us and God.

How wonderful to know that the Lord Who paid the price for our salvation will one day defeat all the powers of evil in the world and establish His kingdom. Until that time comes, let's serve Him in this sin-tainted world in which we now live. Let's make sure He is Lord of our life.

# ℌsalm 111

I LOVE the tenth verse of Psalm 111, which says, *"The fear of the LORD is the beginning of wisdom."* Have you ever really wanted to have wisdom? The place to start acquiring that wisdom is by fearing the Lord or having a deep respect based on awe. Our God **is** *awesome*, and if we feel that awe deeply, we will want to respect Him and put Him in a high position in our lives.

What is *wisdom*? "It is the body of knowledge and principles that develop within a society, or the quality of having experience, knowledge and good judgment." Wisdom involves accumulating knowledge but goes beyond simply knowing facts. Wisdom is having the understanding of the facts to correctly interact in your world.

The verse continues, *"a good understanding have all they that do his commandments"* (v. 10b). We obtain the understanding that gives us wisdom from following and doing God's commandments. And to do them, we need to know them. We learn them from God's Word. A study of the Bible is important in giving us wisdom because God's commandments are sure, as stated in verse seven. Verse eight adds, *"They stand fast for ever and ever, and are done in truth and righteousness."* Since we find so much untruth and unrighteousness in the world today, having an infallible source that we know has the truth and gives us righteous principles to make decisions by is so important.

Let's develop wisdom by fearing the Lord and sharpen our understanding by basing the wisdom we receive on His commandments. Let's stand fast on His true and righteous Word and use it as a foundation in our lives.

# Psalm 112

VERSE FOUR says, *"Unto the upright there ariseth light in the darkness."* *Upright* means "honest, responsible, moral." I want to take a more in-depth look at these three qualities, which are sadly lacking in our society today.

### Honest

We hear so many lies and half-truths that we do not even know who or what to believe anymore. But people should know that because we are Christians, we will tell the truth and they can trust us completely.

### Responsible

No one seemingly wants to take responsibility for their actions any more. We blame our mistakes or shortcomings on someone or something else. Murderers are not to blame for their actions because it is the fault of their environment. Robbers are not to blame for stealing because they are poor. I have seen advertisements and videos for various weight-loss products or programs, and several of their promos start out saying, "It's not your fault you are fat." Obviously, I understand

234 | GERRI JOHNSON

that health issues or hormone problems can affect weight, but a blanket statement that no one is at fault if he or she is overweight is simply not true. The truth is, most people do not want to accept responsibility for their actions.

## Moral

Society is straying farther and farther from the moral principles on which our country was founded. People reject God because they do not want to be morally responsible to a Creator. The home is being destroyed because moral integrity is disappearing.

Watching these traits disappearing from our society is sad, but that disappearance does not give God's people license to follow the same path. This verse contains a promise to those who live an upright life before God. When things seem dark, God sends them light. However dark things may seem, there is a light at the end of the tunnel.

Just as the upright do not need to fear the darkness because God will send Him light, verse seven says He will not be afraid of evil tidings. The upright man can know that whatever God allows in His life is for His good, so He does not need to be afraid of any situation that may come. *"His heart is fixed, trusting in the LORD"* (v. 7b).

Let's walk uprightly and fix our eyes on the Lord, trusting Him in everything.

# Psalm 113

THIS PSALM starts and ends with the phrase, *"Praise ye the Lord."* Verse three says, *"From the rising of the sun unto the going down of the same the Lord's name is to be praised."* This verse suggests strongly that praising God is very important. But what does "to praise Him all day" actually mean?

I think praising involves our attitude. We need an attitude of gratitude and thanks. Then we will be in a frame of mind to praise Him for whatever comes in our lives—whether it seems good or bad to us.

Being grateful for the good things that come our way is easy, but what about the things we don't like? Even they have a purpose, so we need to accept and praise God for them.

I'll be honest, praising Him during the testing times is not always easy for me. I tend to be quick to look at the negative side of things. Many times I park my car on the street, and when I return, the car in front of it or behind it, or both, appear to be parked very close to mine—so close I'll never get out. I start thinking very negative thoughts about the owners of those cars. *Why can't they be more considerate and give me just a little room to get out?* Then, as I get closer, I see that I have plenty of room! I have to retract my negative thoughts and ask God for forgiveness.

How much better it would be if I simply concentrated on the positive. I could thank God for the fact that I have a car to drive. If the other cars really were close, I could thank God for the patience He wants to teach me. I could maintain an attitude of praise instead of grumbling.

Verse five says, *"Who is like unto the LORD our God, who dwelleth on high"?* The answer, of course, is no one. If we concentrate on the greatness of God and all that He does for us in our lives, it will be easier to be positive rather than negative. Being positive, in turn, will help us have an attitude of praise from morning to night.

Let's keep our attitudes positive. Let's strive to praise the Lord all day long.

# Psalm 114

IN THIS Psalm we can learn a lesson from nature. The psalmist mentions three miracles that happened as the Israelites left Egypt, heading to the Promised Land.

Their first big obstacle was the Red Sea. Huge cliffs were on each side of them, a huge sea was in front of them, and the enemy was coming up behind them. But God miraculously parted the sea, and the Israelites walked across—not in mud or puddles of water, but on dry ground!

Their next obstacle mentioned, which impeded their entrance into the Promised Land, is the Jordan River. But, again, God parted the waters so they could cross.

While they were in the desert, they needed water, and God caused water to gush out of the rock.

Verse seven says, *"Tremble, thou earth, at the presence of the Lord, at the presence of the God of Jacob."* All of nature trembles at God's power and obeys His voice. The Red Sea and the Jordan River did not say to God, "No, I don't feel like opening up today. I think I will just keep on flowing." The water immediately obeyed the word of God. Yet we, as men, want to argue

238 | GERRI JOHNSON

with God. We think we know what we need better than God does. We should learn a lesson from nature and behave like the rest of God's creation, obeying Him immediately and without question. How much happier we would be if we did, for as our Creator, He knows us and knows what is best for us.

Let's do as nature does and obey God immediately.

# Psalm 115

IN THE first half of this Psalm, the psalmist addresses the idols of the heathen, describing them as having, among other things, mouths, noses, and ears, but lacking in the ability to speak, smell, or hear. Verse eight adds, *"They that make them are like unto them...."* They have no power to help.

When we think of an idol, we often think of a physical image, like a statue or a picture. But the purpose of idols is for worshiping a god, so in a larger sense, anything we put on the same level as God is an idol to us. If fame, money, houses, or cars, represent what is most important, they are idols. Depending on and trusting more in them than in God for happiness makes them idols.

Verses nine through eleven refer to three groups of people: Israel, the house of Aaron, and those who fear the Lord, saying to them, *"Trust thou in the LORD: he is their help and their shield"* (v. 11). Rather than trusting idols, we need to trust in the Lord. When we are trusting in Him, we don't need to depend on any object of this world. He is our all-in-all.

He is our help. He will help us in whatever things He gives

us to do. He is also our shield, an object which is used primarily for protection. He protects us from any onslaughts of Satan or the world.

Let's not make anything in this world an idol. Let's fear God and trust Him, allowing Him to be our help and protection. Then we will see God's blessing on our lives.

# 𝔓salm 116

T HE PSALMIST starts by declaring, *"I love the LORD, because
he hath heard my voice and my supplications. Because he
hath inclined his ear unto me, therefore will I call upon him as
long as I live"* (vv. 1, 2). He continues saying that he faced trouble
and sorrow and was brought very low, but when he called on the
Lord, the Lord delivered him. These verses could be a description of our lives as well. We are living in a sin-cursed world, and
so often we face problems, difficulties, and sorrows. The question is, how do we react to the issues that come into our life?

Some people love God as long as things are going well, but
as soon as problems come, they blame their difficulties on God
and turn from Him.

The psalmist, on the other hand, after facing what he
called the sorrows of death and the pains of hell, called upon
the name of the Lord. During the times of trouble, we need
God the most; it is not the time to turn away from Him. We
all face difficulties, and God is the solution for all of them. Instead of turning from God, the psalmist called Him gracious
and merciful (v. 5).

Verse ten gives the psalmist's secret in two words: *"I be-lieved."* We can't understand why some things come into our lives, but we can believe that God knows best and that He will help us.

One thing that comes into people's lives and can cause a wrong response is the death of a loved one. Of course, death will cause grief. The stages of grief are normal, but God gives grace to work through them if we ask Him.

Verse 15 is a wonderful verse: *"Precious in the sight of the LORD is the death of his saints."* The Lord is taking that person to be with Him in a world without pain or sadness. The problem, of course, is on our side because we will miss that person. But if we accept God's will, He gives grace for each situation.

The psalmist said in verse 17 that He would offer the sacrifice of thanksgiving. A sacrifice is often hard to make, but if we give thanks for all God brings in our life, He will bless us. Let's do as the psalmist and love the Lord and thank Him for His work in our lives.

# 𝔓salm 117

IN THIS shortest chapter in the Bible, we are instructed in both verses to praise the Lord. Praise is an expression of admiration or approval.

When we admire someone, we often look up to the person as an example of someone we wish to emulate. Unfortunately, nowadays many people, especially young people, tend to admire and idolize the wrong types of people. The choice might be a movie star or a popular singer. The person may possess some type of talent, but that talent is not being used to make a lasting contribution to society. Many times these "idols" also have dubious moral character and are not good role models to copy.

If we look at the characteristics and attributes of God, showing Him admiration should be very easy. He is holy, loving, patient, good, and forgiving to name only a few of His admirable traits. How much better it would be for us to focus our attention on Him and emulate His positive qualities.

Verse two spotlights one of those qualities: His merciful kindness. Because God is merciful, He often shows us undeserved kindness. Do we remember to thank Him and praise Him? Because we admire that quality, do we try to show it to others?

Verse two also mentions that His truth endures forever. What an admirable quality! Do we try to be always truthful in our life?

The other part of praise is voicing approval. When God answers a prayer in the way we want or gives us a huge blessing, showing our approval is easy. Praise Him for the answered prayer. But what if He answers a request with a "no" or allows hardships and difficulties in our lives? Are we still ready to praise Him, showing our approval of what He is doing in our life?

Let's focus our admiration and approval on God and what He does in our life. Let's praise the Lord at all times.

# $\mathfrak{P}$salm 118

THIS PSALM begins and ends with the same verse: *"O give thanks unto the LORD; for he is good: because his mercy endureth for ever"* (vv. 1, 29). These two verses contain three thoughts about thankfulness.

**First, we are to give thanks.** Did your parents ever remind you, "Don't forget to say thank you"? When someone does something for us, thanking them is polite and correct. Your parents may also have made you sit and write a thank you note for a gift you received. Perhaps you even had to learn to write a thank you letter in English class at some time. Showing our thanks is courteous and so important. How much more important it should be to give thanks to God!

**Secondly, we are to give thanks *"for he is good."*** Everything God does is good because goodness is an attribute of His. Even what seems bad to us is for our good. God is all-knowing, so in knowing the future, He knows what will be best for us.

**Thirdly, we are to thank Him *"because his mercy endureth for ever."*** This reason is even mentioned three more times in the next three verses. What an important thought! We often do not deserve His mercy, but He still shows us His mercy over and over. There is no end to His mercy!

Since we are to give thanks to the Lord, verse 24 gives us a beautiful reason to do so: *"This is the day which the LORD hath made; we will rejoice and be glad in it."* Each morning when we wake up, God is the One Who gives us another day. Start the day thanking God for the day. What the day will bring does not matter. It is from the Lord, so we need to rejoice and be glad.

Let's give thanks to the Lord for His goodness and mercy. Let's start each day rejoicing and being glad for whatever He will bring our way.

# ℘salm 119

T HIS CHAPTER is the longest chapter in the Bible, and nearly every verse makes reference to God's Word, which means the Bible is very important! In these 176 verses, His Word is called testimonies, ways, precepts, statutes, commandments, judgments, word, law, and ordinances.

The psalmist described in many ways how he related to God's Word. He *"walked in," "trusted," "kept," "respected," "took heed to," "praised," "meditated in," "sought," and "remembered"* it—to name only a few of the verbs used.

Several verses give us important lessons to learn from the Bible.

Verse nine says, *"Wherewithal shall a young man cleanse his way? by taking heed thereto according to thy word."* We will walk in the correct path and keep our lives clean if we pay attention to His Word.

Verse eleven, *"Thy word have I hid in mine heart, that I might not sin against thee."* Memorizing God's Word will help to keep sin out of our lives. Even Jesus recited Scripture to Satan when Satan tempted Him.

Verse 105, *"Thy word is a lamp unto my feet, and a light unto my path."* What is one item we always take if we are camping or will be walking in the dark? A flashlight, of course! We would trip and fall without it. Even so the Scriptures give us the light we need to guide us when our way seems dim and unclear.

Verse 71, *"It is good for me that I have been afflicted; that I might learn thy statutes."* The psalmist realized that problems were good because they helped him get in God's Word! When everything goes well, it is easy to rely on ourselves. But when problems come, we realize we need God. Verse 107 builds on this idea: *"I am afflicted very much: quicken me, O LORD, according unto thy word."* The problem brought the psalmist to God's Word, and God's Word quickened Him. His heavy load was lightened, and He received renewed strength.

Let's allow God's Word to penetrate every area of our lives. Let's keep it, seek it, believe it, meditate on it, and let it teach us and give us renewed strength.

# Psalm 120

THE PSALMIST asked God for deliverance from lying lips and a deceitful tongue. Has anyone ever lied about you or at least misrepresented or misunderstood something you said or did? I think we all run into this problem at one time or another.

The psalmist goes on to say that He has lived with those who hate peace. In today's world we can see the same thing. People may talk about wanting peace, but they cause strife and division by their hateful or divisive words.

Peace will not prevail in the world between nations or between people with different points of view until Jesus returns and establishes His reign of peace.

Verse seven says, *"I am for peace: but when I speak, they are for war."* That statement seems so true today, especially in the political arena. People actually try to cause strife. They are at war with the opposition, trying to make their point of view dominant.

But that verse is also true in our personal lives. People will cause division and hurt us with their words. It will happen. The

250 | GERRI JOHNSON

important thing is how we react. Returning hateful or angry words will only fuel their fire. We need to learn to turn the situation over to the Lord and ask Him to work His will.

Sometimes a little truth might be present in what is said against us or at least something we can learn from the situation. We need to ask, "Is even a small point of what is being said truthful? Should I consider changing or doing something different?" If so, do it and thank God for the lesson learned. If not, accept the situation as a way to grow in the Lord.

Give any rights you think you have to the Lord and ask Him to help you grow from the situation. Turn your "enemy" over to God. Pray for him, do good to him, and ask God to help you love the person. Easy? No! The right thing to do? Yes!

Let's strive to live in peace with those who do not act peacefully. Allow God to work in your life and theirs.

# Psalm 121

VERSE 2 declares, *"My help cometh from the LORD, which made heaven and earth."* I am always asking my husband to unscrew tight lids for me. I need help from someone stronger than I. Asking a small child to help me would be foolish because he would not have the necessary strength.

When I need help with difficulties in my life, I can come to the Lord. He created everything and certainly has the power to help! He also has the resources to help because everything belongs to Him.

Verse three says He will not allow our foot to be moved. He can hold us firm. Watching someone slipping and sliding on ice on a winter day can be hysterical to watch, but being in that situation is not fun—especially if an injury occurs. We will not slip and slide in life if we are trusting in the Lord. The verse also reminds us that God will not sleep! No matter what time of day or night we need Him, He will be awake to hear!

This verse reminds me of how Elijah mocked the false prophets who were praying to their god for fire to burn the sacrifice with no response. He told them to call louder because maybe their god was sleeping! When Elijah prayed, God answered immediately. Our God is never asleep!

Verse five says God is our shade, and verse six says the sun will not smite us by day. God will protect us from harm. When our daughter was about six months old, we went to the zoo on a cloudy day and walked around with her in her stroller for several hours. That night the sunburn we did not realize she was getting became visible. In fact, the burn was so bad, the blisters began bleeding, causing her sleeper to adhere to her skin. We were not even aware of the danger because the sun did not seem strong. If we had kept her in the shade, she would have been protected. God is our shade to protect us from the dangers of life—even when we do not realize they are there.

Verse seven says, *"The LORD shall preserve thee from all evil: he shall preserve thy soul."* He protects our lives from danger, and He protects our soul from hell. Let's remember where our help comes from and trust Him with our daily lives as well as with our soul.

# Psalm 122

VERSE ONE says, *"I was glad when they said unto me, Let us go into the house of the* LORD.*"* The Jews made yearly trips to Jerusalem to celebrate certain feasts. The temple—the house of the Lord—was in Jerusalem. Although this Psalm is referring to the Jews going to Jerusalem, we can apply its truths to our lives.

Are we glad when we go to the house of the Lord—our church? When Sunday morning comes around, are we excited to think of going to church, or do we dread it? Would we rather roll over in bed and spend the rest of the morning sleeping? I will admit that I am not really a morning person, so I guess I don't ever relish the thought of having to get out of bed. But once I am up, I am glad to be going to church.

Maybe you think going once a week is okay, but you don't make a habit of going to any other scheduled services. We should be glad to be in all of the services of our church.

The church services do several things for us. We get to be together with other believers, which allows for both communion and encouragement between members. We get to praise God with our singing and perhaps be blessed by special music.

Then we get to hear the preaching or teaching of God's Word. While we should read our Bible at home, the pastor can clarify questions we might have on material we did not fully understand or give special encouragement or help.

Let's do as the psalmist and be *"glad when they said unto me, Let us go into the house of the Lord."*

# Psalm 123

VERSE ONE says, *"Unto thee lift I up mine eyes, O thou that dwellest in the heavens."* The psalmist was looking for help, and he knew to look up! Where do we look when we want help?

**Many people tend to look to themselves.** They don't want to depend on anyone else. They think they can or should try to do things on their own. They want to "pull themselves up by their own bootstraps." Some even think depending or relying on someone else shows weakness.

**Some people realize they can't do something on their own and need help with a problem or situation.** However, they look to others, often to people who do not live by Christian principles. They seek counsel from ungodly people.

Obviously, both of these sources are lacking. The psalmist looked **up**, and that is where we should look—up to God. Looking to God does not mean we cannot seek or use the help of godly men or try to do things to help ourselves, but these avenues of help should only be after we first call upon God to ask for His wisdom and guidance.

Verse two gives the example of the eyes of a servant looking to His master and of a maiden looking to her mistress. These examples are of an inferior position looking to a superior, which is exactly our position with God. We are to wait upon God until He shows His mercy to us. We constantly need God's mercies, and as we wait on Him, He will show us His mercy.

Let's realize God's superior position over us, and as a maid waits on her mistress, let's wait upon God. Let's trust Him and turn to Him, rather than relying first on ourselves or others.

# Psalm 124

BOTH VERSES one and two begin, *"If it had not been the Lord who was on our side..."* We could really end that phrase with many truths. If it weren't for the Lord and His dying on the cross, we would not even be saved. If He were not on our side, Satan would defeat us, and we would not have peace and contentment in our lives.

But the thought the psalmist is expressing is that those who do not have the Lord on their side will be overwhelmed by the Enemy. He uses the illustration of being overwhelmed and overcome by water. Calm or slow flowing water can be beautiful and refreshing. But if that water gains power from flooding, it can cause great destruction.

We once had flooding where we were living, and our entire kitchen and living area of our apartment were covered with water. We even had water flowing out our backed-up commode like a fountain—a very disgusting one. We literally swept and shoveled out the water all morning. We actually were in the process of packing to move back to Brazil after furlough. We moved boxes and belongings off the floor as soon as possible and were able to minimize some of the damage. Our situation was disheartening but nothing compared to what damage great floods cause.

Thankfully I have only seen extensive flooding damage in video coverage! We know water can be a very destructive force, and the psalmist wants to paint the picture of what being without the Lord on our side would be like.

Then He changes the imagery in verse seven to that of a bird escaping from a snare. When we accept the Lord as our Saviour, we escape the snare of Satan. We are freed from the future condemnation of hell and from the present control of Satan in our lives. That freedom is not due to our goodness but to the Lord's work in our lives.

Truly, we can say with the psalmist in verse eight, *"Our help is in the name of the LORD, who made heaven and earth."* Let's remember to call on His name to avoid the floods of life and to be delivered from the snares of Satan.

# Psalm 125

VERSE 2 SAYS, *"As the mountains are round about Jerusalem, so the LORD is round about his people from henceforth even for ever."* *"His people"* in this verse may be referring to Israel, but I believe many truths in the Psalms can be applied to the lives of all Christians. Jerusalem really is surrounded by mountains. In fact, everything in the Holy Land seems to be on or near a mountain. They are not like the huge, snow-capped mountains of the Rockies nor the rolling green hills of Kentucky, but they are fascinating in their own way—with very little grass and many small rocks.

As those mountains surround Jerusalem, so God surrounds us with His protection. He is at our side and will be there forever. We know He will be there with us until the end of our journey in this life.

In verse four, the psalmist says, *"Do good, O LORD, unto those that be good, and to them that are upright in their hearts."* God is with us throughout our life, but if we want Him to do good to us, we need to meet these two conditions.

1) **We need to be good.** Being *good* means "morally right

or righteous." Being good would involve developing God's moral principles in our lives. It would involve all you should do when someone says, "Now be a good girl." Be nice, thoughtful, honest, helpful, loving, and so forth. The list could go on!

**We need to be upright.** This means honorable or honest. To me, being upright focuses more on our inner qualities rather than external actions, although both words are similar in meaning.

Do you want God to do good to you? Then let's develop the qualities of goodness and uprightness. Let's also remember that God is always surrounding us. Let's rest in His presence.

# Psalm 126

ECAUSE ISRAEL had turned away from god to idols, God eventually punished them by sending them into captivity. But this Psalm describes them after they turned back to God. God set them free, and they returned to the Promised Land. It was like they were dreaming, and they were full of laughter and singing.

We do the same thing as Israel did. We might turn to "idols" of this world—like fame, money, a big house, or a new car. Anything we make more important than God in our lives can become our idol. God may try to get our attention and call us back to Him, but like Israel, we often don't listen. So God disciplines us in some way.

God brought Israel back to their land, and He wants to return us to the life of blessing we lose when we turn from Him. If we will simply turn back, He will also fill our lives again with laughter and singing. Let's seek Him and let Him fill our lives with laughter.

One way to have joy in our lives is to share the gospel with others. The last two verses contain a promise to us if we are trying to serve Him. We should be telling others about His salvation, and the psalmist says, *"They that sow in tears shall reap in joy. He that goeth forth and weepeth, bearing precious seed, shall doubtless come again with rejoicing, bringing his sheaves with him."*

The last thing Jesus told us as He returned to heaven was to preach the gospel to the whole world. If we try to do that and share the news of salvation with others, God will fill us with rejoicing. It may seem difficult at times, but our tears will turn to joy as we continue to serve Him.

If we have wandered away from the Lord, let's return and allow Him to bless us again. Then let's share the gospel, trusting His Word that says our tears will be turned to rejoicing.

# Psalm 127

I LOVE VERSES three through five of this Psalm, perhaps be-cause they talk about children. I have five, plus one in heaven I did not get to know.

*"Lo, children are an heritage of the LORD: and the fruit of the womb is his reward. As arrows are in the hand of a mighty man; so are children of the youth. Happy is the man that hath his quiver full of them: they shall not be ashamed, but they shall speak with the enemies in the gate."*

I will not address the subject of how many children to have. That decision is one for each husband and wife. Some people would like to have children, but that is not God's plan for them. We should never judge others, either thinking they have too few or too many children.

God says children are a heritage. An older definition of *heritage* is "a special or individual possession," and children are certainly special. He also says they are a reward.

Then He compares the children to arrows of a mighty man. A skilled archer can do much with his arrows, but that skill comes from much training. If we were not trained in our homes as we grew up, then we need to study God's Word to know how to train our children.

The world today, which has listened too much to modern godless psychology, no longer believes in training and discipline. The child is left to choose what he wants to do and is given no limits. A child reared in that way will not be a good arrow to make a positive mark in society.

Because many parents no longer train and control their children, children are often viewed in a negative way. People ask, "You have **how many** children?" as if having more than one is a curse. How sad!

I have been asked at times how I "survived" rearing five children. I will not say I had an easy task. Rearing children takes effort, determination, and time to teach and train them in God's way. But I can testify that the time invested is well worth the effort. My children are certainly a reward from the Lord. Let's train our children in God's way, and they will be a blessing to us and the world.

# 𝔓salm 128

T HIS PSALM begins *"Blessed is every one that feareth the LORD; that walketh in his ways"* and then cites several ways they will be blessed. Notice, two conditions are given.

The first condition is to fear the Lord. One definition of *fear* is "reverential submission." Fear with the idea of being afraid or in terror would only apply to someone who has not yet accepted the Lord as Saviour. Christians do not need to fear His condemnation; thus, we have a reverential awe of Him that should cause us to want to submit to His will for us.

The second condition is to walk in his ways. Another definition of Biblical *fear* is "inducement to obedience and service," which leads us to walk in His ways. If we have awe and respect for our great God, we should want to serve Him and follow Him. We need not only the right attitude but also the right action for God to bless us.

The second verse gives us three ways God will bless.

1) *"Thou shalt eat of the labor of thy hands."* This verse is directed mainly to the head of the home. His work will prosper, and he will be blessed financially to be able to provide for the family.

2) *"Happy shalt thou be."* *Happy* means "feeling or showing pleasure or contentment." When we seek the pleasures of the world, happiness is short-lived. But when we are serving God, we feel real contentment.

3) *"And it shall be well with thee."* I think this segment covers many areas of our lives—our health, our general sense of wellbeing, our emotions, our relationships. We will be able to say, "All is well."

Verse six lists one final blessing: *"thou shalt see thy children's children."* We are promised a longer life. Let's fear the Lord, serve Him, and see the blessings He bestows on us.

# Psalm 129

"MANY A *time have they afflicted me from my youth, may Israel now say: Many a time have they afflicted me from my youth: yet they have not prevailed against me*" (vv. 1, 2).

This Psalm specifically refers to Israel, but the principles can be generalized for all of us. We also are "afflicted" with problems. Our enemy is not another nation, as with Israel. Our enemy is Satan, and he wants to afflict all Christians in any way possible to keep them from serving God.

Satan wanted to prove to God that Job would not serve Him when life did not go well. God allowed Satan to bring many trials into Job's life, but not once did Job turn his back on God. Neither did God turn His back on Job! Even as He allowed difficulty, He was always at Job's side. In the end, God blessed Job with double of what he had lost.

God does not promise to double our material goods when we stay faithful through trials as He did for Job, but He will stay with us like He did for Job and like He did for Israel. The psalmist said they were afflicted, but the key is the next phrase: "*yet they have not prevailed against me*" (v. 2).

Sometimes Satan will use the unjust and wicked to cause trials in our lives, but verse four tells us, *"The LORD is righteous: he hath cut asunder the cords of the wicked."* God, in His righteousness, will fight for us. The wicked may try to hold us in their power and destroy us, but God cuts their cords. They have no power to control our lives.

When we have problems and trials, let's remember that our enemy cannot win over us when we keep our confidence in the Lord. Let's remember that the Lord is righteous, and He will win over the wicked. The victory is already ours!

# Psalm 130

Ave you ever felt like you were in the "depths of despair" or at least down in the dumps? That is how the psalmist felt. He starts this Psalm: *"Out of the depths have I cried unto thee, O Lord."*

But the psalmist knew where to turn. In verse two he asks the Lord to hear his voice and his supplications.

In the next verses the psalmist indicates his reason for feeling low. He reflects that no one could stand before God if God would not forgive our iniquities. But after that negative thought, he gives the positive truth that God does forgive our sins. He forgives us when we come to him for salvation and when we trust what Christ did for us on the cross. But we will only be perfect when we receive our new body in heaven, so we are going to continue to sin at times. If we bury those sins in our lives and do not confess them, they can pull us down in the dumps and eventually cause real feelings of despair. We need to confess those sins to regain our communion with God. We do not lose our salvation, but we definitely lose communion with Him.

If we daily examine our lives and confess any sin, we can

270 | Gerri Johnson

keep from having that feeling of despair. Verse five adds an additional way that we can be helped. The psalmist says, *"and in his word do I hope."* God's Word gives us hope.

Let's make God's Word an important part of our life. Let's read it, study it, meditate on it, and memorize it. The Bible can help keep us from being down in the dumps or in the *"depths of despair."*

# 𝔓salm 131

T HE PSALMIST begins by asserting that He is not haughty or
lofty. *Lofty* means "acting like you are high above everyone else." *Haughty* has nearly the same meaning—"arrogantly
superior and disdainful." Do you know someone like that? No
one likes to be around that type of person.

We may not be like that all the time, but have you ever let
a little of that kind of attitude peek out? Some synonyms for
*haughty* include "proud, stuck-up, self-important, condescend-
ing, smug, or scornful." Have you ever exhibited some of those
characteristics?

At times we all may be a little self-centered and preoccu-
pied with ourselves. We are more concerned with our own af-
fairs than those of others. We can resolve that problem if we remind ourselves that the Lord tells us to love others as ourselves.
Focus on others.

We may also sometimes think that we are a little better
than someone else. We all have talents and abilities that God
gives us. We may actually be able to do something better than
someone else, but that is no reason to be proud or stuck-up.

272 | GERRI JOHNSON

The other person probably has something he or she can do better than us! Even if that is not the case, God created each of us and wants us to love each other as we are. This bubble of superiority can soon be burst if we stop to think of what we all are before God. The Bible says our righteousness is as filthy rags. If so, how can I consider myself better than someone else?

Verse two says, *"Surely I have behaved and quieted myself."* Let's do as the psalmist and behave with the humility of a little child. Let's quiet the spirit that wants to feel superior and accept everyone as an equal.

# ℙsalm 132

THE MAJORITY of this Psalm addresses how David wanted to build the house of the Lord and later how God promised that His descendants would always sit on the throne.

I want to focus on a phrase cited in two verses. Verse 9 says, *"and let thy saints shout for joy,"* and verse 16 says, *"and her saints shall shout aloud for joy."*

A *saint* is simply someone who has trusted the Lord as Saviour. *Saint* comes from a root word meaning "holy." When Jesus saves us, we are made holy through His blood. All our sins are forgiven, so in God's eyes we are made holy.

If we have been forgiven and made holy, then we certainly have a reason to shout for joy. But what makes that joy last? How can we always have joy in our hearts?

When I think of the word *joy*, I always think of the illustration of what brings joy using the word *joy* itself. It illustrates priorities in who should be most important in our lives:

J—Jesus
O—Others
Y—Yourself

Unfortunately, many times we fail to put our priorities in that order. Instead, we often invert the order, thinking of ourselves first, others second, and Jesus in last place. And that, my friend, is the reason why we do not always have joy. If we put our priorities in the correct order, making Jesus most important in our lives, then serving others, and putting ourselves in last place, we are much more likely to have His abundant joy in life.

Let's shout for joy because we are saved. Then let's put our priorities in the right order to keep that joy bubbling in our lives.

# ℙsalm 133

"**B**EHOLD, HOW *good and how pleasant it is for brethren to dwell together in unity!*" (v. 1). What a lovely truth that is! Have you ever fought with your sister or brother? If we have a sibling, most of us would have to admit we had our differences with them. I was older and never wanted my sister to tag along and play with my friends and me.

But most of us would also admit that we would stand up for our siblings if someone tried to bully or hurt them. That's what family does. By the way, my sister and I are usually far apart physically, living on different continents, but now I would always want to have her around if possible!

Other church members are part of our spiritual family, and it is important for us to live together in harmony and unity. Verse two says living in unity is like *"the precious ointment upon the head, that ran down upon the beard, even Aaron's beard."* In those days, showers like we have today were nonexistent. The general people did not take baths every day like we do. A scented oil on the head was pleasant and refreshing. Uniting together with other Christians at church should also be refreshing. It should be a time of communion—not of division.

In verse three, the dew is also used as a comparison to our unity. The morning dew is also refreshing to see on the grass and plants.

Let's strive for unity as we get together with fellow believers. Let's make our fellowship sweet and refreshing.

# Psalm 134

THE FOCUS in this short Psalm is on blessing. The first two verses tell us to bless God, and the last verse is asking for a blessing from God.

I read four definitions of *bless* that would describe our blessing God:

1) **"To call God holy."** God certainly is holy, and we will especially realize this truth if we compare God to our unrighteousness, which He compares to filthy rags. There is no way we can really fathom His holiness, but we should stop to think about it as well as dwell on the other marvelous attributes of our holy God.

2) **"To praise God."** Certainly, after meditating on God's holiness, we should praise Him for all He is. We all like to be praised, and God deserves praise much more than any human being. We can praise Him in prayer or in song. Listening to Christian songs and hymns can help us think about His goodness, and we can sing along in an audible voice or in our hearts.

3) **"To thank God for His mercies."** When we think about God's holiness and compare it to our sinfulness, it is easy to see

278 | Gerri Johnson

His mercy to us when He saved us. He also shows us mercies each day as we walk with Him. We need to thank Him daily, even many times a day, for all His mercies on us.

4) **"To glorify."**- To *glorify* means "to praise and worship," or "to describe or represent as admirable." We can glorify God by going to church and worshipping Him. But we can and should also glorify Him by how we represent Him in our lives. When we live a life following God's principles found in His Word, then our life glorifies Him before others.

Let's praise God for His holiness, thank Him for His mercies to us, and glorify Him in our lives as we serve Him.

# Psalm 135

VERSE ONE tells us three times to praise the Lord, and then verse three adds, *"Praise the LORD; for the LORD is good: sing praises unto his name; for it is pleasant."*

We are to praise the Lord because He is good. *Good* can mean "morally excellent, righteous." Our perfect God **is** certainly good, and we should praise Him for this attribute. But God also **does** good to us. Sometimes He gives us good things that are desirable and pleasant. Sometimes He gives us situations or allows circumstances that are for our good, although we might not consider them pleasant. We should praise Him for what He **is** and what He **does** because whatever He chooses is always good.

The second part of verse three tells us to sing His praises. Music is an integral part of our lives. We automatically react to certain sounds or rhythms, like automatically tapping our feet without even realizing it when we hear a song. My husband was at a printer's office once, and one of the machines was making a "swoosh, swoosh" sound. Another man standing at the counter started tapping the keys of a keyboard to the rhythm of the machine. His innate musical chord had been struck! Let's use the musical instinct that God gave us to sing His praises.

You might not think you have a voice for singing solos at church, but singing solos is not necessary to praise God. You can sing in the shower if you enjoy that time. You can sing hymns and spiritual songs any time you are alone. You can join your voice with others as you join in the congregational music at church. But sing to the Lord. Think about the words you are singing. You are not really praising God if you sing by rote without even thinking about the meaning of what you are singing.

I thought the last phrase of the verse was interesting: *"for it is pleasant."* Hearing us praising Him is pleasant to God and also pleasing to us. Have you ever felt a little "down" or discouraged, but you heard a peppy song that perked up your spirits? When you feel down, put on some Christian music and listen to it. Let the pleasantness uplift your spirit! (The music we enjoy can be lively but should not be sensual.)

Let's praise the Lord because He is good and sing unto His name.

# 𝔓salm 136

E VERY VERSE of this Psalm ends with the phrase *"for His mercy endureth forever."* Obviously, the psalmist was trying to say that God's mercy never ends! The first two verses tell us to give thanks to the Lord. In these verses the main reason to give thanks is for His mercy.

But verse one gives yet another reason: *"for he is good."* Verses two and three confirm that we are giving thanks to the God of gods and the Lord of Lords. The remainder of the verses demonstrate His goodness.

Verses four through nine tell of the great wonders He performed by His wisdom in creation: the heavens, the earth, the waters, the sun, the moon, and the stars. God was merciful to us in giving us such a wonderful world.

In verses 10 through 22, we see the marvelous ways God worked in taking the Israelites out of Egypt and leading them to the Promised Land. If we look at our lives, we can see how He also works marvelously and mercifully on our behalf.

Verses 22 through 23 could certainly be related to Israel, but they also apply to us. God sees how low and helpless we are

282 | Gerri Johnson

in our sin and redeems us "from our enemies" (v. 24). Satan is our greatest Enemy, and the Lord delivers us from his power when we are saved. But God wants to also deliver us from the "enemies" who attack us in our day-to-day lives.

Verse 25 reminds us that He gives *"food to all flesh."* In other words, He supplies our physical needs. After citing all these benefits, the psalmist reminds us in verse 26 to give thanks to the Lord.

Let's heed that command and give thanks to the Lord for all He does. Let's especially remember His great mercy to us.

# 𝔓salm 137

"**B**Y THE *rivers of Babylon, there we sat down, yea, we wept, when we remembered Zion.*" This sad Psalm is about Israel while they were held in captivity in Babylon. Their captors wanted them to sing, but they said they had no song. All they could think about was what they had enjoyed in the past.

They did have reason to be sad, since they had been forced to live in a land that was not theirs. As I read these verses, I cannot help but feel they were having a pity party. They could not change their present situation, so focusing on the past would not help them. In fact, dwelling in the past was only making them more miserable.

We often do the same thing when we are in a situation we do not like. When we have problems or difficulties, focusing on the negative will only make us feel worse. We need to try to find something positive on which to focus our attention.

The situation with Israel could have been avoided if they had listened to God. They were turning from God, and He had warned them of the consequences of their actions, but they did not listen. God often warns us in His Word of the consequences of not following His principles or walking in His ways. But we often do not even spend time in the Bible to notice His various warnings.

God spoke to Israel through many prophets, but the people still did not listen. The pastor or another man of God may try to warn us of God's discipline when we do not listen to Him, but we often want to continue in our own way. We could avoid many sad situations if we would listen to warnings and decide to walk in God's way.

When we are in a sad situation, let's not have a pity party. Rather, we need to focus our attention on something positive. If we have turned from God's way, let's turn back and let Him control our lives. Best of all, let's obey God and walk with Him to avoid many heartbreaking situations in the first place.

# Psalm 138

WHEN OUR kids were all still at home, we went to a camp-ground our church owned to have a picnic and play games. No one else was there, so we started playing a game of soccer. The game was well underway when we noticed that our youngest son was missing. We called his name and started looking all over the grounds for him but did not see or hear him. Finally, we found him trapped in a fence-post hole that was being dug. His arms were stretched above his head. Though he had been calling for help, we did not hear Him. He had to wait patiently until we finally found him.

Verse three of this Psalm says, *"In the day when I cried thou answeredst me."* We do not have to wait until God notices we have a problem or until He can hear us when we call on Him. He knows our situation before it happens, and His ear always hears. How wonderful that we have a God who hears and also answers when we pray!

The last part of the verse says, *"and strengthenedst me with strength in my soul."* When we need strength, He is there to supply it. My favorite verse in the Bible is Philippians 4:13, which says, *"I can do all things through Christ which strengtheneth me."* The strength we need comes from God. Our son needed someone with strength to lift him out of that hole. We need strength to have victory over problems and situations in our lives. As with the psalmist, we know that God is the One Who gives that needed strength.

I love verse eight, which says, *"The LORD will perfect that which concerneth me...."* When we call on Him and rely on His strength, He will work in our life to make us better. We will never be perfect until we get to heaven, but He is working on perfecting us more and more each day. You have probably heard or even quoted the saying, "God is not done with me yet." But He keeps working away at us!

Let's call on Him, depend on His strength, and daily let Him keep perfecting us more and more.

# Psalm 139

Verses one through six show us the omniscience of God. He knows all about us! He knows when we stand, sit, or lie down. He knows our thoughts and every word that comes out of our mouth. If we want to keep something secret from someone, we whisper or talk when they are not around. But we cannot keep any secrets from God! He knows what we will say even before we say it.

Verses seven through ten reveal the omnipresence of God. He is everywhere! If we want to flee from God, it is impossible. But if we are following Him, verse ten is an assurance: *"Even there shall thy hand lead me, and thy right hand shall hold me."* Wherever we go, He will guide us and hold us firm like a mother who's holding the hand of her small child to keep the child from slipping.

Have you ever played hide-and-seek in the dark? When I was a child, we used to do that outside in the evening after the sun went down. Finding someone in the dark is hard! Verses 11 and 12 tell us that even the dark cannot hide us from God. The darkness and light are the same to Him.

God knows all about us; there is nowhere we can hide from Him because He is everywhere and sees all; even the darkness does not hide us from Him. Then verse 16 tells us He knew us and saw us even before we were formed.

Realizing all these truths, the psalmist did something very important in verses 23 and 24. He said, *"Search me, O God, and know my heart: try me, and know my thoughts: And see if there be any wicked way in me, and lead me in the way everlasting."* The psalmist wanted God to examine his thoughts and attitudes. Then he asked God to examine his way. We need to ask God to do the same—examine what we think and examine what we do. We need to forsake the sin God uncovers and ask Him to lead us in His way.

Let's realize God's greatness and ask Him to search us, cleanse us, and lead us in His path.

# ℙsalm 140

IN THIS Psalm the author is asking for deliverance from evil and wicked men. He mentions also the violent and the proud man. In today's world, men are seemingly moving farther and farther away from God's principles, often not wanting anything to do with God in their lives. People with ideas completely opposite of biblical principles want to push their ideology on society. We definitely need to ask for God's help against the wicked, as the psalmist did in His day.

> "I said unto the LORD, Thou art my God: hear the voice of my supplications, O LORD. O GOD the Lord, the strength of my salvation, thou hast covered my head in the day of battle" (vv. 6, 7).

These verses show us several qualities of God. First, the psalmist said, "Thou art MY God." He is a personal God, interested in each of His children. He will hear our voice.

He is our strength. We don't need to rely on our own strength to win the struggle. We need only to depend on Him.

The psalmist said that God covered his head. In most states, motorcyclists are required to wear a helmet. Why? Because a head injury is life-threatening and generally fatal. Our brain controls all the various parts of our body and needs to be protected. God gave the most vital protection in the day of battle. He will also protect us in the battles of life with complete protection.

In light of this Psalm, the psalmist knew God would give the victory. Verse 13 says, *"Surely the righteous shall give thanks unto thy name: the upright shall dwell in thy presence."* When God gives us the victory, we need to remember to give thanks. We can be thankful for the assurance that when the struggles of this life are over, we will live in God's presence forever.

Let's remember it is the God of the universe but also our personal God Who is fighting for us. Let's rely on His strength, thank Him for the victory, and relish the fact that in the end we will spend all eternity in His presence.

# ℙsalm 141

THE PSALMIST asks God to hear His prayers in the first two verses, and then in the next two verses he gives two important requests that we should also want answered in our life.

"*Set a watch, O LORD, before my mouth; keep the door of my lips*" (v. 3). We all have doors on our houses. They are to keep out the wrong people but also to keep the right people in and protected. If you have an indoor dog, the door keeps him in when you do not want him to escape. Even so, we should have an invisible door to our lips to keep things in that we do not want to escape. Some examples of what to keep in are words of anger, complaint, defamation, and any words that would hurt people.

The psalmist also asks to set a watch. Companies hire guards to watch their buildings. In Brazil, men will ride a circuit around blocks of houses and charge a small price to keep watch on those houses for protection. They, of course, want to keep out the robbers, while we want to keep our harmful words contained.

"*Incline not my heart to any evil thing, to practice wicked works with men that work iniquity: and let me not eat of their dainties*" (v. 4). The psalmist asked to keep his heart pure. One way to help do that is to avoid close friendships with those whose works are not good. The psalmist talks about eating their dainties—time spent eating together, which usually means a friendship with them. We should be kind to everyone but not spend a lot of time fellowshipping with those who are not Christian and do not walk in God's ways. Otherwise, their ways will rub off on us.

You do not put a good apple with bad ones to turn the bad ones good, and if you put a bad apple with good ones, it can turn the good ones bad. The psalmist wanted to avoid bad influences on his life.

Let's pray for God to give us victory, strive to keep wrong words from escaping our lips, and keep wrong friends or acquaintances from destroying our lives.

# 𝕻salm 142

Have you ever been so overwhelmed that you felt like you did not know where to turn? The psalmist said in verse three, *"When my spirit was overwhelmed within me, then thou knewest my path."* He was overwhelmed, but he realized that God already knew all about the issue. So the psalmist knew where to turn.

Verse five says, *"I cried unto thee, O Lord: I said, Thou art my refuge and my portion in the land of the living."* The psalmist turned to the Lord. As long as we are still alive and walking this planet, the Lord will be our refuge. That thought is a comfort when we are going through difficult times.

But in the midst of these verses, the psalmist says something I think is very sad at the end of verse four: *"no man cared for my soul."* God is all we need, but it is nice to know that there is some human who cares about us too!

But turning things around, do we take our eyes off ourselves, and look to see if someone needs US to care about THEM? We can speak a kind or encouraging word to someone who is passing through difficult times. We can bake them a cake or some cookies or offer to give a listening ear. What would you want someone to do for you? Do that for someone else. Don't let anyone you know be able to say, "No one cared about me."

Although the psalmist was saved, the phrase *"no man cared for my soul"* can also make us think of the unsaved. How many people around us have never heard how Christ can forgive them of their sins and save them? How many people have we shown that we care for by telling them the most important thing in the world—how to have peace with God?

When we are overwhelmed, let's remember to turn to the Lord. But let's also remember to look around us and show a fellow Christian who is going through difficulties that we care. Let's show the lost we care by sharing the gospel with them.

Let's not let anyone we know be able to say, *"No man cared for my soul."*

# $\mathcal{P}$salm 143

THE PSALMIST is beaten down by his enemies and feels overwhelmed and desolate, but he knows where to find help. In verse one he asks God to hear his prayer.

In verse five he mentions three things that he does:

1) *"I remember the days of old."* Remembering can be bad if we are looking back and want to relive the past. But it is good if we are looking at how God worked in our life before and trusting that He will do it again.

2) *"I meditate on all thy works."* The more we meditate on what God has done for us in the past or on the truths we see in His Word that He did in Bible times, the more we will be confident of how He can work in our lives today and deliver us from our difficulties.

3) *"I muse on the work of thy hands."* Muse means "to think of something carefully and for a long time." Since the psalmist mentions the work of God's hands, I think of His creation. When we spend time looking at nature and how marvelously we ourselves are made, we realize how powerful and wonderful God really is. He certainly possesses the power to help us.

Verse six tells us the psalmist thirsted for God as in a thirsty land. Have you ever been really thirsty, perhaps after a race or physical activity or on a very hot day (with no air conditioning)? You want a drink more than anything and even become focused on satisfying that desire. That is the way in which the psalmist sought God.

The psalmist sought deliverance, but he asked for a very important request. In verse 10 he said, *"Teach me to do thy will."* That is the secret for having God always nearby and ready to help. We need to want to do His will, not ours. Doing that will also help us avoid many difficulties in life!

Let's remember what God has done in the past, meditate on what He has done already in our life, and think about His glorious works. Let's have a thirst for God and always seek to do His will.

# Psalm 144

IN VERSES seven and eight, the psalmist asks God to deliver him from *"the hand of strange children; Whose mouth speaketh vanity, and their right hand is a right hand of falsehood."* *"Strange children"* would indicate a people who do not serve the Lord. God always tells us in His Word to be separate from the ungodly.

The psalmist mentions two things these people did. The first was to speak *vanity*, i.e., "excess pride in oneself." We should not belittle ourselves and consider ourselves worthless, but neither should we be "full of ourselves" and think we are better than others. These people without God were proud, thinking they did not need God. The psalmist wanted no part of them.

The second thing the psalmist mentioned about them was their right hand of falsehood. I think of this as dishonesty and living a deceitful lifestyle. We see much of this in the world today, and it certainly does not please God.

The psalmist realized God could not bless him if he mingled with these people. The end result would likely be his corruption.

298 | Gerri Johnson

From verse 12 on, the psalmist mentions several benefits for avoiding this type of person and following God.

The first benefit would be seen in our sons and daughters, who would grow up to be honorable. The next was prosperity; the land would give fruit, and the animals would multiply and be strong. The third benefit would be contentment. The psalmist said there would be no complaining in the streets. What a wonderful world that would be!

The psalmist ended by saying, *"Happy is that people, that is in such a case: yea, happy is that people, whose God is the LORD"* (v. 15). The wicked who do not want to turn to God will always be in the world. But if we will personally make the Lord our God, we will be happy.

Let's turn from vanity and dishonesty. Let's make sure the Lord is our God. Then we will be happy.

# ℙsalm 145

Ⅴ ERSE 3 says, *"Great is the L* ORD*, and greatly to be praised; and his greatness is unsearchable."* We should be praising God for His greatness that can be seen all around us, yet is so great there is no way to understand or fathom it.

Although we cannot understand the depth of His greatness, we should be passing it on. Verse four of this Psalm says, *"One generation shall praise thy works to another, and shall declare thy mighty acts."* Have you ever had a job to do and put it off or shirked it? The job in this verse is to praise God's works and declare His mighty acts, and I am sure some believers are following this verse. But I think many of the past generation have shirked this duty, perhaps even thinking, *it was not their job!*

A new generation has come up, and many of this generation want nothing to do with God and even declare He does not exist. Instead of declaring the wondrous things God has done in creating our marvelous universe, they believe and teach that everything came about by evolution.

We need to pick up the slack and begin passing on the truth to our children and the next generation of the mighty acts God has done. The psalmist in the next verses also talks about God's attributes—honor, majesty, goodness, and righteousness. Verse eight reminds us, *"The Lord is gracious, and full of compassion; slow to anger, and of great mercy."*

Perhaps we have not passed these truths on to the next generation because we ourselves do not stop to think about them. We are so busy living our lives that we don't meditate on God's greatness.

Let's stop shirking our duty and pass on the truths of God that we have learned. Let's talk of His marvelous works and His wonderful attributes.

Let's make verse 21 true in our lives: *"My mouth shall speak the praise of the Lord."*

# Psalm 146

Do you want to be happy? Verse five says, *"Happy is he that hath the God of Jacob for his help, whose hope is in the* Lord *his God."* Have you ever hoped for something and then were disappointed because you didn't get what you were hoping for? The disappointment certainly doesn't make you happy.

The psalmist says our hope should be in God, and then he gives a list of what God does that should make us happy.

First, He reminds us that our God made heaven and earth. He is the all-powerful Creator. He also *"keepeth truth for ever"* (v. 6). Have you ever wondered whom or what you should believe? That can be very frustrating. But neither God nor His truth changes. We find His truth in the Bible, and we can trust every word!

Verse seven says He helps the oppressed, gives us our food, and *"looseth the prisoners."* We can be prisoners of our sins, our emotions, or our circumstances. But if we look to the Lord, He can free us.

Verse eight says, He *"raiseth them that are bowed down."* Have you ever felt like the weight of the world is on you? It's hard to bear, isn't it? But remember Who our God is. He can raise us up and release that pressure.

Verse ten says, *"The LORD shall reign for ever...."* He is not someone who helps us today but will not be around tomorrow. He is Lord forever and is ever present to help us and give us relief and joy.

Let's remember Who God is and all He does for us. Let's be happy in Him!

# Psalm 147

VERSE ONE says praise is good, pleasant, and comely. *Good* means "that which is right." God is certainly deserving, so it is right for us to praise Him. *Pleasant* means "bringing happy satisfaction." This would apply to both the giver and the receiver. God is pleased, or happy, when we praise Him. Giving Him praise should please us and make us happy. *Comely* means "attractive" but also "suitable or agreeable." Praising the God of the universe for all He does for us is certainly suitable.

I love verse three, which says, *"He healeth the broken in heart, and bindeth up their wounds."* When something happens that breaks our heart, it certainly causes a wound. If we had nowhere to turn, it would take a long time for us to heal, or possibly we would walk through life with a gaping wound in our being. But when we turn to God, He closes our wounds. We will still hurt, but healing will come.

We know He can help us because verse five says, *"Great is our LORD, and of great power: his understanding is infinite."* I have heard of people who go from doctor to doctor for physical help and find no solution to their problem. Doctors are

304 | GERRI JOHNSON

human, and human knowledge is faulty. But if we go to God, the great physician, there are two reasons He can help us: His power and His understanding. He has power to do anything, and He understands everything, so He knows how to help us. After all, He created us and everything else in this universe!

So let's turn to Him. Verse 11 says, *"The L*ORD *taketh pleasure in them that fear him, in those that hope in his mercy."* He wants to heal our wounds and guide us through this life. So let's come to Him in reverent awe of Who He is and trust in His mercy because He loves us and wants to help us.

# ℘salm 148

THIS PSALM starts and ends with the command, *"Praise ye the LORD."* The Lord first asks His angels and hosts to praise Him. Then several aspects of nature are mentioned—the sun, the moon, the stars of light, the heavens, and the waters—basically a summary of the first part of creation week.

It may seem strange to ask for inanimate creation to praise God, but Jesus said if men did not praise Him, He could make the rocks do so. I think nature sometimes has more "sense" than humans!

Verse 5 says, *"Let them praise the name of the LORD: for he commanded, and they were created."*

Verses seven through ten continue to mention other natural phenomena like fire, hail, snow, and vapor that God put into action and finally the animals—beasts, cattle, creeping things, and flying fowl. All were created by God, and all are asked to praise Him. Even if they do not speak with a loud voice, they praise God simply by their presence. The wonders of nature cannot be fathomed. If we stop to analyze them, they produce an awe for their Creator.

306 | GERRI JOHNSON

Finally, in verses 11 and 12, humans are commanded to praise God, starting with the highest authority of kings and including young and old alike.

Verse 13 tells why we should praise Him: *"Let them praise the name of the LORD: for his name alone is excellent; his glory is above the earth and heaven."* The word *excellent* indicates "something above everything else." God is way above His creation, and His glory is above earth and heaven. That is reason enough to praise Him.

Let's be aware of the awesomeness of His creation and praise Him for the wonders He has created and given us to enjoy.

# Psalm 149

VERSE FOUR of this Psalm says, "*For the LORD taketh pleasure in his people: he will beautify the meek with salvation.*" Too many people today think of God as either nonexistent or impersonal. They picture Him as a God out there somewhere Who put the world in motion and then left it to itself, with no individual interest in the people inhabiting it. What a completely false image of God! This verse says the Lord takes pleasure in us. He cares about each of us individually. What a wonderful thought!

I see a second truth in that verse. Have you ever considered yourself less than beautiful? Maybe you would like to change some things about your appearance. This verse talks about beautifying someone. Who is beautified? The meek are beautified with salvation.

Before we come to the Lord for salvation, we must first realize that we are lowly sinners. We need to come to Him in meekness, recognizing that we can do nothing to save ourselves. When we put our trust in Him, something happens. We are beautified. No, the shape of our nose or the color of our eyes or the general shape of our body does not change. But something happens inside us that causes a transformation no beauty technique could accomplish.

Let's thank God because He cares for each of us as individuals. Let's praise Him for the beautiful transformation He makes in our lives when we accept Him as our Saviour. Let's allow verse six to become true in our life: *"Let the high praises of God be in their mouth...."*

# Psalm 150

EVERY VERSE of this Psalm tells us to praise the Lord. Verse one tells us to praise Him in two places—His sanctuary and the firmament. His sanctuary today could be compared to the church. One reason we go to church is to praise and worship God with other believers.

To me *firmament* gives the idea of nature—all that God created. So, everywhere we go, we can look and see God's handiwork. Nature should make us stop and think of His power and cause us to praise Him.

Verse two specifically says to praise Him for His mighty acts and excellent greatness. Nature and the world around us should naturally cause us to think of these things and praise Him for His greatness. We can see His mighty acts in nature, but we should also be able to see them in our lives. The greatest act He performed in our lives was to save us. We need to constantly praise Him for our salvation.

He does great acts for us each day. He keeps our hearts beating. He gives us food, raiment, and shelter. He gives us family and friends. We should praise Him for that.

But has He ever done a REALLY great act for you? Perhaps you or someone close to you was healed from a serious illness. Perhaps someone who was barren now has a child. Perhaps a wayward child came back to the Lord. When these great acts happen, we praise the Lord. But how long does it take us to forget about what God did in our life or in that of a loved one? We need to constantly remember the great things He does and praise Him.

Let's be faithful in church to praise the Lord there. Let's notice the glories of nature and praise God for them. And let's remember the great acts God performs and always praise Him.